THE
SAILING
COOK BOOK

THE SAILING COOK BOOK

KITTY HAMPTON

WILLOW BOOKS
Collins
8 Grafton Street, London
1985

Willow Books
William Collins Sons & Co. Ltd
London · Glasgow · Sydney
Auckland · Toronto · Johannesburg

First published in Great Britain 1985
© Kitty Hampton 1985

Jacket photography by Paul Kemp
Illustrations by Brenda Armit

Hampton, Kitty
The sailing cook book.
1. Cookery, marine
I. Title
641.5'753   TX840.M7

ISBN 0 00 218169 X

Filmset in 11/14pt Linotron Century Schoolbook
by Rowland Phototypesetting Ltd
Bury St Edmunds, Suffolk
Printed in Great Britain.

CONTENTS

ACKNOWLEDGEMENTS

I would like to express my very grateful thanks to the following people who have contributed their recipes, advice and experience to this book: Maralyn Bailey; John and Jean Bassett; Chay and Maureen Blyth; Eve Bonham; Edward and Penny Bourne; Andrew Bray; Chris Butler; Glynn Christian; Gabriel Clay; Major Richard Clifford, Royal Marines; Peter de Savary; Daphne du Maurier; Dame Mary Donaldson, DBE; Major Frank Esson; Richard and Maura Fanshawe; Clare Francis; Ann Frazer; Major Robin and Mrs Priscilla Gamble; Commander David Gay, Royal Navy; John Gore-Grimes; Geoff Hales, MBE; Liz and Anne Hammick; Desmond Hampton; Rachael Hayward; Tim and Mary Heywood; Laurel Holland; Jeff Houlgrave; Ralph Hammond Innes, CBE; Dame Naomi James, DBE; Sir Peter and Lady Johnson; Robin Knox-Johnston, CBE; Sue Lloyd-Evans; Margot Lovel; Lieutenant John Martin, South African Navy; Jock McLeod; Colin and Rosemary Mudie; Martin Muncaster; Robert Nickerson; 'Winki' and Georgina Nixon; Her Grace Lavinia, Duchess of Norfolk, CBE; Elizabeth Ogilvy-Wedderburn; Nicholas Parsons; Bill and Hazel Perks; Peter and Joan Phillips; Pat Pocock; Libby Purves; John Ridgeway; Mike Ritchie; Jeremy and Fiona Rodgers; Nigel Rowe; Angela Sainsbury; Mike and Suzi Scneideman; Des Sleightholme; Major Ewen Southby-Tailyour, Royal Marines, OBE; Dr Nigel Southward; Andrew Spedding; Major Peter Thompson, Royal Marines; Valentine Thornhill; Peter and Patricia Trumper; and Gustave Versluys.

I would also like to thank Betty Hitchcock, the publishers' home economist for her help and advice in testing many of the recipes, Westerly Yachts Ltd for the use of *Konsort* and *Sea Hawk* in the front cover photograph, and Colins Willow who made the whole project possible. Last and not least, my long-suffering family who have been patient guinea pigs over the years.

KITTY HAMPTON, JANUARY 1985

FOREWORD

The Jubilee Sailing Trust, which I have been involved with since the beginning, is doing marvellous work.

The aim of the Trust is to bring the physically handicapped and the able-bodied together as a team through the medium of a specially-equipped offshore sailing vessel. Invariably the physically handicapped develop the will to win while the able-bodied discover the contribution to society that the physically handicapped can make, if given encouragement to do so.

Over the last two summers the Trust was able to put their aims into practice and to prove their value by chartering and specially equipping the *Soren Larsen* – and will repeat this in 1985. They take blind, deaf, spastics, epileptics, those in wheelchairs and so on, together with the able-bodied, between the ages of 16 and 69. The rehabilitation results have been startling and have enabled many handicapped people to fit themselves more easily into everyday life and into employment.

However, the *Soren Larsen* is not entirely suitable and so it has been decided to build at James Cook's Yard, Wivenhoe, Essex, the *Lord Nelson*, a specially-designed sailing vessel incorporating all the features necessary for the physically handicapped. This will be capable of carrying double the numbers that the *Soren Larsen* can take and will last some 50 years.

Keel laying of the *Lord Nelson* took place on 19 October 1984 and the vessel will be launched in late 1985. HRH The Prince Andrew is to name her in early 1986 in time for the sailing season that year. Eventually it is expected that she will sail to the Caribbean to take on local handicapped from the USA during our winter season and so work throughout the year.

I am therefore delighted that Kitty Hampton has produced this wonderful book which not only makes cooking at sea so much easier but also dedicates the proceeds to the Jubilee Sailing Trust.

Lavinia, Duchess of Norfolk
Vice-Patron of the Jubilee
Sailing Trust

INTRODUCTION

When all sailors cast off the shackles of the shore, whether it be for a passage of only a few hours or for a voyage that may take them many months, they share one thing in common and that is the pleasure they derive from being at sea. I am delighted that the royalties from this book will help towards providing sailing facilities for the disabled. The aim of the Jubilee Trust is: 'For the physically handicapped and able-bodied to share in the challenge of crewing a ship at sea.' The fact that over 50 people have contributed recipes to this book has shown how much yachtsmen appreciate these aims. Although many of the contributors are my personal friends, they have willingly allowed themselves to be bullied into remembering just how they prepared that superb meal which was the highlight of their cruise or into recalling the creation that saw them through a particularly bad spell of weather, as well as giving me many ideas and much useful advice.

My other aim in compiling this book was to provide what I hope is a practical cookery book. When at anchor or sailing in near calm conditions cooking on board is really no different from cooking at home. There is less working space (which often turns you into a far tidier chef than normal), and there are fewer appliances such as freezers, microwave ovens and food processors, but that should not mean that there is any drop in the standard of meals produced. After all, the main meal of the day is often the only time of the day the crew is gathered together and so it should be a social and enjoyable occasion.

Good food is part of the tradition of our seafaring nation. Samuel Pepys was responsible for the victualling of the Navy for some years and wrote: 'English-men, and more espicially [sic] seamen, love their bellies above everything else, and therefore it must be remembered in the management of the victualling of the Navy, that to make any abatement of them in the quantity or agreeableness of their victuals, is to discourage and provoke them in their tenderest point, and will sooner render them disgusted with the King's service than any other hardship that could be put upon them.' It is certainly true to say that a major cause of mutiny at sea was discontent with the food and drink.

Although I have divided the recipes into three sections, they are not really hard and fast as I'm sure sea-going cooks will realize. The sections are as follows:

Beaufort Wind Scale 0–2, calm to light breezes   These recipes are more suitable for calm and settled conditions as they tend to be rather more complicated to prepare or require fresh ingredients that you may not have to hand while on passage. Many of the dishes could be made and frozen at home before being taken down to the boat.

Beaufort Wind Scale 3–6, gentle to strong breezes   On passage the kind of meal you feel like preparing will depend on a number of different factors such as the size of your yacht, whether it is mono- or multi-hull, the wind direction, and your own ability to juggle with pots and pans as well as where you are. Handing the helmsman a stuffed, red-hot potato while he's coping with a shy spinnaker reach could, as they say, ruin your entire day! Generally speaking, the larger the yacht the more working space there will be available and she is also more likely to have a steadier motion. However, whatever the size of the yacht, a hard slog to windward produces very different conditions below than when running downwind. On the other hand, given enough sea-room and assuming you're not racing, you could always heave-to while dinner is being prepared.

Beaufort Wind Scale 7–12, moderate gales to hurricanes   Cook in time for Force 9. This is what boy scouts will be prepared for in advance. It is quite rare that you will not have had some indication that bad weather is approaching and so as well as making sure that all gear on deck is secured and prepared for a blow, make ready in the galley. Make a larger stew than normal which could last for longer than one meal, fill up the thermos with hot soup, make some sandwiches, top up the 'munchie' box and you won't be caught with your oilies down.

Whether cruising or racing, I hope this book will encourage you to experiment a little in the galley and that, for you, good sailing and good eating will not be incompatible.

THE GALLEY

Galley Lay-out   The most important feature of the lay-out of any galley is that everything should be within reach on either tack. Use one easily accessible locker for tea, coffee, milk, sugar, cocoa and instant soups. It is also a good idea to keep there a box of 'munchies' such as chocolate, dried fruit and nuts so that the crew can help themselves without disturbing anyone else. I find it useful to have what I call a ready-to-use locker in which I stow such basic ingredients as rice, spaghetti, herbs and spices, as well as enough tins and packets for the next couple of days. This saves diving under the saloon seats and rummaging in the bilges more than is absolutely necessary.

The Stove   The stove is swung on gimbals and should have both a crash bar and a galley strap to protect the cook. The fiddles around the top of most cookers tend to be too low to be really effective and should not only come at least halfway up the sides of your pans, but should also have movable bars so that they can be clamped in position. If you find that your stove swings about too much in rough weather try damping the action by placing a heavy weight high up in the oven. If you put it too low the pendulum effect will simply be increased.

Keeping food cold   Some yachts are equipped with a fridge which is very useful for perishable foods like milk, butter and fresh meat, although its power consumption can be quite a drain on the batteries if it is left on all the time. However, if it is kept full you need to run it for one hour a day only to ensure that the beer, so I am told, is sufficiently cold! Personally I have never owned a boat with a fridge and find that the water temperature in Northern Europe is sufficiently low to keep most things cold in the bilges. Most yachts, however, have some form of cold box. If you pack it with frozen food in boxes and replace each box as you take it out with a piece of polystyrene of the same shape, its insulation will be greatly improved.

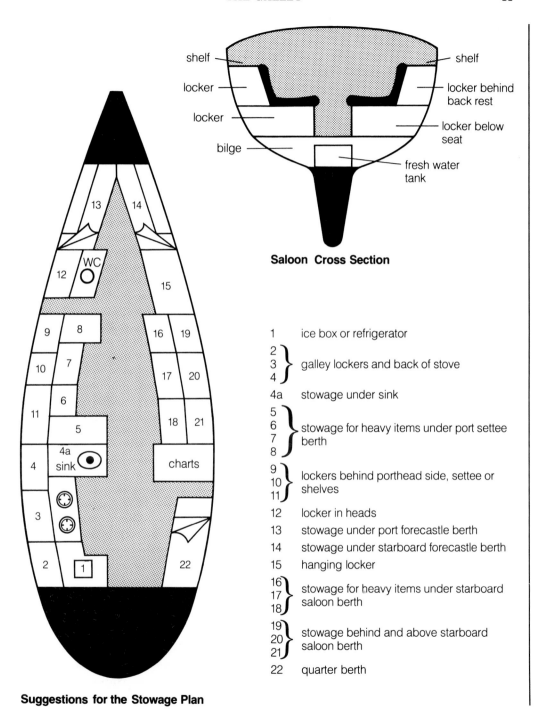

Saloon Cross Section

shelf
locker
locker
bilge

shelf
locker behind back rest
locker below seat
fresh water tank

Suggestions for the Stowage Plan

1	ice box or refrigerator
2 3 4	galley lockers and back of stove
4a	stowage under sink
5 6 7 8	stowage for heavy items under port settee berth
9 10 11	lockers behind porthead side, settee or shelves
12	locker in heads
13	stowage under port forecastle berth
14	stowage under starboard forecastle berth
15	hanging locker
16 17 18	stowage for heavy items under starboard saloon berth
19 20 21	stowage behind and above starboard saloon berth
22	quarter berth

Cooking fuel   The majority of yachts are fitted with gas stoves and the bottles are usually stowed in a self-draining locker on deck. For safety, the gas should be turned off after use at both the bottle and at the tap close to the stove where the flexible hose joins the copper piping. Every galley should have a fire extinguisher to hand as well as a fire blanket. In severe weather it is sensible to wear chest-high oilskin trousers to protect yourself when cooking.

Using salt water   A salt water pump can be extremely useful. Washing up in salt water is perfectly all right and in fact a great many yachtsmen seldom do anything else, particularly if away for a long time or during a long-distance race. If you are not trying to save your fresh water, a final rinse in it helps keep the rust at bay. Ordinary washing-up liquid works as well as any 'fancy' brand of salt water soap and can be used as hair shampoo.

PRESERVATION AND STOWAGE

Stowage   At the start of the season make a plan of all the stowage space available and keep a chart handy showing where the stores and gear are stowed. Apart from being a memory jogger it saves having to explain to new crew members where everything is kept. I also try to keep a stores' list, crossing off each item as it's used. Not only will it show you what was or was not popular in the tin line but it can save hours of ferreting around the bilges in pursuit of that tin of *foie gras* you were sure you had left.

Tinned Foods   Heavy foodstuffs such as tins, should be stowed as low as possible. Most yachts have locker space under the saloon seats for this purpose. The danger of lockers flying open in bad weather is very great. More than one person received quite severe head injuries when missiles were flung out of their lockers during the 1979 Fastnet Race.

Unfortunately, few bilges are absolutely dry and tins will become rusty. They are still usable but should the tin begin to bulge or spurt out its contents, then discard it at once. At the end of the season it is sensible to remove all the tins. When buying the tins make sure that they are not dented.

Marking the Stores   If you are considering a long voyage, Robin Knox-Johnston advises removing the labels (loved by bilge pumps), coding the tins with paint and then varnishing them. Use an easily recognisable abbreviation when coding them.

Planning the Stores   When drawing up the stores' list before an expedition to the supermarket or Cash and Carry try to include as many variations as possible. Many of the contributors to this book have come up with suggestions. Some say never buy more than two of any one variety of tin or foil packet, and others suggest that you plan to have an Indian meal (curry), Italian (pasta), Greek (dolmades) and so on every three or four days. The choice of pâtés and other delicacies now available in tins is so much wider than it used to be that it is possible to have a more varied diet on board. Here are a few suggestions on which foods last well on board to help you in planning your stores:

PRESERVATION

Bread	Bread will keep for longer if it has not been frozen. Granary and wholemeal will stay fresh for about ten days and sliced bread for about seven days. Some hard-baked rye breads will not go stale for about a month.
Butter	Wrapped in aluminium foil and stowed in a cold place, for example the bilges, it will keep for a minimum of four to six weeks. Tinned butter will keep for at least a year.
Cakes	If you want to keep moist fruit cakes or Parkin, put them on a thick slice of bread and wrap in aluminium foil.
Cheese	Vacuum-packed cheese will stay fresh for several months as long as the seal is not broken. Whole truckle Cheddars keep well even in warm and moist conditions. Slice off the top and use it as a 'lid'. Peel down the outer cloth as you eat the cheese and fold it back over the cheese as you use it up.
Dehydrated Meals	These are a useful stand-by and can also be added to a 'pot luck' stew to stretch it further.
Dried Fruit	Raisins, sultanas and apple rings last well and are extremely useful.
Eggs	These will last for a very long time without any treatment at all provided that they have not been refrigerated or chilled. So, trying to preserve them by rubbing them with Vaseline or by any other trick is not only messy but unnecessary. Eggs are not often kept in refrigerators in British shops, even in supermarkets, but in some countries they are and will therefore last only two weeks.
	A number of contributors to this book report of having kept eggs fresh for at least four months. One handy tip is to turn them over at least once a week to prevent the yolk

from settling at one end and consequently leaking out of the shell.

Fish   If you have caught more than you can eat in a day, try smoking or pickling them.

Foil Packs   These are easier to stow than tins and also lighter in weight. Usually more expensive than tins but they are very popular with long-distance ocean racers. They are available from some stores or by mail order.

Fruit   Apart from being unbruised and as fresh as possible, it is essential that the fruit has not been chilled if you want to keep it for a long period. The only way to avoid this is if you visit one of the many 'Pick your Own' farms or make friends with your local supermarket manager. My own local supermarket is most helpful and will always ensure that I get the freshest produce possible.

Hard fruit such as apples, oranges, grapefruit, lemons, limes, melons and unripe mangoes will keep better than the softer fruits such as pears, peaches and plums. Green bananas will not ripen so quickly if you wrap them in brown paper and stow them somewhere dark. Bring them out a few at a time.

Garlic Bulbs   Will last up to six weeks at least.

Herbs   On a long trip fresh chives, parsley, mint and tarragon can be grown in plastic containers and mustard and cress will flourish on kitchen paper.

Meat   Smoked hams last almost forever. If they should go mouldy, scrape off the mould and hang them in the rigging on a dry and sunny day. Salt beef and pork will keep for months, if not years, in brine. It is possible to buy vacuum-packed meat and some butchers will arrange this for you if your supermarket hasn't any in stock. As long as the seal is not broken and the meat is kept out of the light it will stay fresh for up to a month but do check the date stamp. Beef and lamb will keep slightly longer than poultry, but only for five to six days. If meat begins to smell 'high' wash it well in a mixture of one-third vinegar to two-thirds water.

Pasta

It is extremely useful to keep spaghetti and other types of pasta on board throughout the season. They keep well in a dry place.

Poultry

Fresh poultry should be eaten within two to three days, especially if it is not kept in a refrigerator.

Pulses

Kidney beans, lentils and chick peas all last well but must be kept dry.

Rice

Again rice keeps and, if you buy it in large packs, it is a good idea to divide it into separate airtight containers.

Salad Stuffs and Vegetables

Hard-packed lettuces such as Webbs or Icebergs will last longer than the soft variety. Cucumbers will only stay fresh if you remove them from their plastic 'sock'. Carrots, peppers, aubergines, sweetcorn and tomatoes last well. Buy tomatoes and avocadoes in various stages of ripeness.

Hard, tightly-packed cabbages will last for at least five to six weeks. It is interesting to note, however, that five days after being picked, up to 90 per cent of their Vitamin C is lost. Potatoes are high in Vitamin C and even after four months' storage still contain 20 per cent milligrams per 100 grams.

Onions keep well but if they start to sprout use the sprout as fresh chives. Freeze-dried peas, string beans and dehydrated onion are an extremely useful stand-by. Curried or pickled vegetables stored in containers make a pleasant change and go particularly well with cold meat.

SPROUTS

These are easy to grow on board and are very nutritious. They enliven any diet and can be eaten raw or cooked. Add them to salads or sprinkle them over some soup just before serving. Alfalfa is delicious in omelettes or stir-fried with soy sauce. How long these beans take to sprout will depend on the temperature. In hot, damp conditions they will grow very fast indeed but cold weather will slow down their growth.

Aduki	Slightly more expensive than the others and slower growing
Alfalfa	Fastest growing and will grow 14 mm (½ in) in two days. Also inexpensive
Mung	Takes three to five days to grow. Has a very good taste and is good stir-fried
Mustard & Cress	Both good grown beyond the sprouting stage to leaf stage, very good in sandwiches
Soya	Has a strong flavour
Wheat	Not the best in flavour

To grow them you will need:
1 large jam or coffee jar or any wide-necked jar
1 porous cloth; the toe of an old stocking is ideal
1 rubber band or piece of string

Put one to two tablespoons of seeds into a jar; be careful not to put in too many. Stretch the stocking over the top of the jar and secure it with an elastic band or some string. Pour through enough warm water to cover the seeds easily and leave overnight in a warm place. In the morning, drain off the water through the cloth and rinse with a little fresh water. Drain again and place the jar upside down so that the water continues to drain off. Seeds left in water will not sprout. Rinse out every morning for two to three days, or until ready to eat.

STORES' LIST

This list is intended as a guide only. Many of the items can be kept on board throughout the season and form the basis of many meals.

Bicarbonate of soda	has a shelf life of six months only
Biscuits, plain	
Butter, tinned	

Cereal or muesli
* according to choice*
Cocoa
Coffee
Cornflour
Curry powder or paste
Dehydrated potato powder
Dried fruits such as
* raisins, sultanas,*
* currants*
Dried milk powder or
* longlife milk*
Eggs
Flour, plain and
* seasoned*   store in airtight plastic containers
Herbs   basil, garlic and mixed herbs come in paste form and are available in tubes. Otherwise keep in plastic containers. Useful herbs are basil, bay leaves, mint, parsley, mixed herbs, rosemary, sage, thyme and tarragon

Lemon juice in plastic
* 'lemon'*
Margarine in plastic
* containers*
Meat extract
Mustard, dried
Oil
Packet soups
Parmesan cheese
Pastry mix   rub 225 g (8 oz) butter or margarine into 450 g (1 lb) plain flour until it resembles fine breadcrumbs. If stored in a plastic container it will keep three to four weeks. Make up with a little water and roll out in the usual way

Pasta
Pickles

Porridge oats

Preserves

Rice store in airtight plastic container

Salt and pepper store in airtight plastic container. If you are using a mill, make sure that all the moving parts are made of plastic

Spices store in airtight plastic containers. Chilli can be bought in paste form in tubes. Particularly useful spices are cayenne, chilli, cinnamon and whole cloves

Sugar, white and brown

Stock cubes, chicken and beef

Syrup

Tins tomatoes are very handy but according to choice

Tomato ketchup and purée

Vinegar

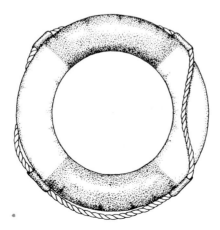

GALLEY EQUIPMENT

Some people manage to survive with just a pressure cooker, frying pan, corkscrew and a tin opener. However, if you have the space, none of the following items will go amiss.

1 pressure cooker the main reason why these are so popular on board is that the lid can be clamped on so that even if the pot flies off the stove, the contents remain in the pot rather than all over the cook or in the bilges. They are also very economical on fuel

1 large saucepan with lid

1 medium saucepan with lid it is possible to buy a 'nest' of saucepans which includes a frying pan and egg poachers

1 small saucepan with lid

1 frying pan

1 grill pan

1 kettle

2 ovenproof dishes

1 baking tray

1 flameproof casserole

1 graduated measuring jug

1 large sharp knife

1 vegetable knife

1 sacrificial knife keep it in its cardboard sheath and make sure it is the only one used heated-up to cut rope with, for cleaning some part of the engine or as a screwdriver. I got fed up with my best knife being returned pointless, filthy and resembling a bent hacksaw blade. Mind you, the dividers make an excellent pick for cleaning out crabs

1 asbestos mat

1 garlic crusher

1 potato peeler

1 whisk
2 wooden spoons
1 slotted draining
  spoon
1 spatula
1 fish slice
1 plastic strainer
1 colander
1 small strainer
1 pr scissors
1 grater
1 chopping board   many yachts have some form of chopping board in-
                            corporated into the galley – if not take your own
2/3 tin openers   like small electrical screwdrivers and foredeck
                            hands, they are never around when you need them!
                            Keep spares well hidden

1/2 cork screws
1 egg timer   not just for timing eggs. More widely used for waking
                            the skipper or remembering the weather forecast

aluminium foil
Cling Film
lavatory paper
kitchen paper

KEEPING SHIPSHAPE

Seasickness There are a few simple guidelines which I feel are worth mentioning on seasickness. Nigel Southward, a keen sailing GP, suggests that in order to obtain maximum benefit from whichever pill you take, start taking them on the evening before sailing. You should also remember to keep taking them regularly. Avoid, if possible, too much rich food and alcohol before departure – it's a shame to have to share your dinner with the fishes as well as being a waste of francs.

Keep an eye on the young or inexperienced crew for the first warning signs which are often constant yawning and a general air of lassitude. Try and encourage anyone who is feeling ill to eat and drink something. Apart from retching on an empty stomach being extremely unpleasant, dehydration is a dangerous side effect of seasickness. Give them plain, preferably wholewheat, bread or biscuits to nibble and as the boat's water supply may not be all that palatable, add some effervescent Vitamin C tablets.

Seasickness is the enemy of cooking at sea. You should know what you are capable of preparing. If going below to boil a kettle is all you can manage without feeling ill, then obviously the best thing is to plan your meals around hot water. Instant soup, bread and cheese, dried fruit and nuts make a sustaining meal. A cook who can produce simple, if cold, food without a green face is preferable to one who manages to produce a hot meal but who infects the rest of the crew with seasickness in the process.

Vitamin Intake Ensure also that there is sufficient Vitamin C in the diet generally, especially in stressful times such as during seasickness or bad weather. Rosemary Mudie and several other of the contributors believe, and I wholeheartedly agree with them, that in winds of Force 7 or over, it is mainly a question of keeping people nourished.

Food is a fuel and it does not have to be hot, though there is something psychologically comforting in having a hot meal or drink in inclement weather. Many boats and crews have been put at hazard because their judgement was diminished by a lack of proper nourishment. It is very easy for your Vitamin intake to suffer, especially in times of stress. As I have already mentioned it is very important to take a wide variety of food, particularly if you are going on a long voyage. Make a note of what people do or don't eat as they may well develop quite odd likings for different flavours, probably reflecting the body's instinctive need for trace elements (such as salt during exceptionally hot weather). A large percentage of Vitamin C and B-complex is lost during cooking either being destroyed by the heating process or leached into the cooking water. To retain as much of the natural vitamins as possible cook rapidly in a small amount of water. If using tinned vegetables, make use of the liquid in soups and stews. On long voyages I would recommend taking a good multi-vitamin tablet once a day. It is unseamanlike to allow yourself to become run-down due to malnourishment.

Scrubbing the Decks Mould and a foul smell of dampness will build up very quickly if the boat is not properly ventilated, lockers not cleaned out and above all, if the 'heads' are neglected. Cleaning these is usually everyone's least favourite chore and the only fair way to see that they do get cleaned out every day is to ensure that everyone takes their turn. Similarly, the galley is an area around which grease and dirt will build up in no time at all if it is left. At the end of the sailing season it is worth while washing the whole of the interior of the lockers and the bilges as well as the head linings with fresh water and a mild anti-fungicide or water and Milton.

First Aid Box A first aid box and manual should be kept in a place known to everyone and should include: seasick pills; aspirin; antiseptic tape; plasters; lint; gauze; surgical tape for burns and cuts; antibiotic powder and TCP. If setting off on a long voyage discuss with your doctor what you should take with you.

Panic Bag A panic bag to take with you into the life raft should be kept within easy reach of the cockpit. If should at least contain: some flares; EPIRB or distress beacon; foil blanket; and glucose tablets. If you are contemplating a long voyage it is best to consult some specialist books for more information on what items the bag should contain.

PREPARATION OF SEAFOOD

Having persuaded the fish to take your bait, the next problem is how to prepare it for the pot. Here are a few guidelines for preparing round fish, flat fish, crabs, mussels, squid and some more exotic kinds of shellfish.

Round Fish (for example, pollack, grey mullet, herring and mackerel)

The fish most frequently caught by yachtsmen is the mackerel which luckily requires little preparation apart from removing its guts. However, other round fish such as the sea bass or grey mullet are not so easy to get ready as they have coarse scales which must be taken off.

To remove the scales: I recommend that you cover your working surface and as much of the surrounding area as possible with newspaper since removing the scales is a messy business and the scales tend to fly everywhere. Then, holding the fish firmly by the tail and using the back of a strong knife, remove the scales by pushing them up the wrong way from tail to head.

To gut the fish: Slit the fish open from the vent up towards the head. Remove the guts and wash the fish well in clean sea water. Remove the head and tail or not as desired.

To bone the fish: Continue to cut the fish from the vent towards the tail, sliding the knife as close to the bone as possible. Remove the head and tail. Lay the fish flat on a board, cut side down, and press along the backbone to loosen it. Turn the fish over and lift out the backbone and any other small bones which may be sticking out. Cut the backbone off at each end using scissors or a knife. Left whole the fish is now ready for a stuffing or it can be filleted by cutting along the top of the backbone and lifting the top fillet right off.

Methods of cooking round fish (1) *baking:* One of the best methods of cooking fish on board is to wrap it in aluminium foil and bake it in the oven. This also reduces the cooking smells. The fish is usually enclosed in foil or greaseproof paper together with wine, herbs or other seasonings and is cooked in its own juices. If you do not have an oven you can prepare it in the same way but poach it on top of the stove in a covered pan of gently simmering water. (2) *grilling:* Slash each side of the fish with three diagonal cuts and grill for 4–10 minutes, turning once after the first side is browned. The skin should be golden brown. (3) *frying:* Very little oil is needed for frying oily fish such as herring or mackerel. I cannot recommend deep fat frying on board except in the calmest of seas or while at anchor; even then use the largest saucepan available and only about 2.5 to 5 cm (1 to 2 in) of oil.

Flat Fish (for example, sole and flounder)

To skin and fillet the fish: Using a sharp knife, make a cut down each side of the fish between the fins and the flesh. Loosen the skin by running the thumb under the flap of the skin. Ease the skin away from the flesh at the tail end and then, with your fingers, pull quickly from tail to head removing the skin completely. Repeat on the other side.

Next, still using a sharp knife, cut the fish down the centre backbone which is clearly visible. Working from the head and keeping the knife close to the bone, cut in sweeping strokes from the right to the left until the fillet is lifted. Turn the fish round and do the same on the other side and then repeat on the other side of the fish until you have four fillets in all.

Methods of cooking (1) *grilling:* Brush with a little oil and grill for about 5–10 minutes, depending on the thickness. (2) *frying:* To shallow fat fry, quickly roll in seasoned flour or even egg and crumb mixture and fry in oil and butter for about 10–12 minutes.

Shellfish

Clams These are available from the Helford River and are delicious stuffed with a mixture of garlic and butter. Rinse the clams in several changes of cold water to rid them of all sand. Place the clams in a large strong pan a few at a time with enough water to cover the bottom of the saucepan. Shake the pan over a high heat for about 5 minutes, or until the clams are open. Take care not to overcook them, though, as they can become very tough.

Crabs (Flat Back or Tourteaux) There is some controversy as to the kindest way to kill a crab or lobster. Plunging them into a large pan of boiling water is, in my opinion, far quicker than the slow death by suffocation which is what happens if you put them into a pan of cold water and bring it to the boil.

Whichever method you choose, simmer the crab for about 20 minutes. If the crab is over 2.3 kg (5 lb) allow it to cool in the water. When cold, drain and turn the crab onto its back, twist off the small legs and large claws and set aside. Push back the tail flap and pull off. Holding the crab firmly with one hand, hook your thumb and first finger of the other hand into the holes left by the claws and pull the body of the crab away from its shell. Remove and discard the gills or 'dead men's fingers'.

In the top of the shell, just below the eyes, is the mouth and stomach sac. Press down on the mouth with your thumb and lift it and the sac out and discard. That's the easy part done!

Cut the body of the crab into two with a strong, sharp knife, then pick out into a bowl all the white meat from the cavities with a skewer. Then crack the large claws, using a mallet or hammer, and carefully remove the flesh from the shell adding it to the rest of the white meat. Crack the small legs, remove the shell and scrape out the flesh.

From the sides of the big shell scoop out with a teaspoon all the brown meat into a separate bowl. Around the edge of big shell is a natural line; press down firmly around the line and it will break away giving a much larger space in which to pile the white meat around the outside and brown meat in the middle. Most restaurants in Brittany serve the crabs open leaving it to you to settle down and pick out the meat yourself with the aid of nutcrackers, toothpick, crusty bread, mayonnaise and some wine – there can be few better ways!

Spider Crab (Arraignés)   With its spikey body and long fearsome legs, it rather resembles some monster from a science-fiction film. Cooked in the same way as the flat-backed crab, it can be a little harder to separate the body from the shell. The crab has little brown meat but the white meat is sweeter and some say more delicate than that of the flat-backed crab.

Cockles   These are found along most of the British coast but particularly at river estuaries and on shallow sandy beaches. If the cockles are in their shells stand them overnight in salted water sprinkled with oatmeal to allow the sand to seep out. Next day, drain, scrub well and put in a saucepan. Pour over enough boiling water to cover and boil for 3 minutes. Drain and remove cockles from their shells.

Cooked like this, they will bear no resemblance to the nasty, vinegary and rubbery cockles loved by some seaside stalls. Add them to a tomato sauce or toss them in butter and garlic. Serve with spaghetti and there you have a meal worthy of the finest restaurants.

Mussels There is something deeply satisfying about scrambling along a rocky shore, bucket in hand, as you gather any number of different shells and shrimps for the pot. The most common find must be the clusters of blue-black mussels clinging to rocks all along the coastline. As yet they are not scarce and a bucketful will provide a delicious and filling meal. Make sure that you pick them from somewhere where they are washed by the tide and not where there is an obvious sewage outlet to the sea.

It is extremely important to wash and scrub mussels in several changes of fresh sea water to rid them of all sand. Jettison any mussels that refuse to shut when tapped sharply. Scrub them with a stiff brush, scraping off any barnacles and pulling off their 'whiskers'.

The simplest method of cooking them is to put them in a large saucepan with a wine glass of white wine or cider. Cover and cook them over a high heat, shaking the pan from time to time to make sure that all the mussels come into contact with the heat. Cook for about 5–8 minutes, or until all the mussels open and discard any that remain shut.

Oysters (Huîtres) Like scallops, oysters were once cheap and plentiful – even to the extent that during Victorian times they were considered to be food for the poor. Nowadays, however, they are in the luxury class. The two most easily recognizable are the round, flattish kind called the *Ostrea edulis*, of which the Colchester, Whistable and Belon are the most famous, and the *Cassostrea angulata* or Portuguese oyster which has a rough and knobbly shell. The latter is less expensive but experts do not consider it to have such a delicate flavour.

To open Hold the oyster firmly in one hand, flat side up, with the hinge pointing away from you. Holding a broad-bladed, strong knife in the other hand, insert the point at the hinge and push firmly into the oyster. Then slide the knife around either side of the shell and lift off the top half of the shell.

To serve The best way to serve oysters is *au naturel* with a squeeze of lemon and plenty of fresh bread and butter plus a bottle (or two) of Muscadet Sur Lie.

Prawns and Shrimps 'If either of these be of a dead, dull colour, have a faint smell, feel slimy, and are limber, they are stale; if their scent be pleasant, and they are hard and stiff with their tails bending strongly inwards, you may conclude that they are fresh and good.' (*Madam Johnson's Present*, 1766)

Scallops   Like oysters, these used to be cheap and commonplace until the twentieth century. They have now become so expensive that they belong to the luxury class. You are unlikely to pick them up from the beach as they live quite deep below the surface of the sand and are usually dredged up by fishermen. They are available in Britain from about November to April.

To open the shell, slide the point of a strong knife between the edges of the shells as close as possible to the hinge. Continue to slide the knife around the edge of the shell to cut the very strong muscle. Separate the fish from the shell, remove the orange coral and set aside. Slice the white meat into half, cutting across the top. Discard all black parts and also the gristly piece of skin around the centre white piece. Wash the meat well to remove all sand. The orange coral is delicious and is cooked with the white meat. Poach in a mixture of one-third water to two-thirds white wine for 3–4 minutes.

Squid   Most of us have eaten squid abroad or even at home in restaurants and no doubt thought them quite delicious. However, the chaotic array of a bucketful of squid is rather a daunting sight and the prospect of cleaning and cooking them not very appealing. But it is not as difficult as it might first seem.

The smaller squid with about a 7.5 cm (3 in) body are the best size for frying while the larger ones are better for stewing and stuffing. Squid have a purplish-red skin which doesn't look very appetizing. In a bowl of fresh water, gently rub away the skin. Pull the head and tentacles away from the body, along with the hard transparent nib-like piece called the pen. Discard the pen and also the ink sac which is attached to the head and found in the soft part of the body.

Cut the tentacles away from the head just above the eyes and set aside. Discard the head and innards. There is a small round cartilage near the base of the tentacles. Squeeze out and discard. Rinse the squid well and cut the body and tentacles into rings.

Winkles   These small black shells are found in abundance all round our coasts and can be distinguished from similar shells by the very obvious sharp point at the top of their shells. In France they accompany most *fruits de mer* along with a cork and a hat pin with which to flick off their hard, round 'front doors' and to winkle out the creature inside. Boil them in plenty of fresh, clean water with a bay leaf for about 10 minutes. Drain and allow to cool.

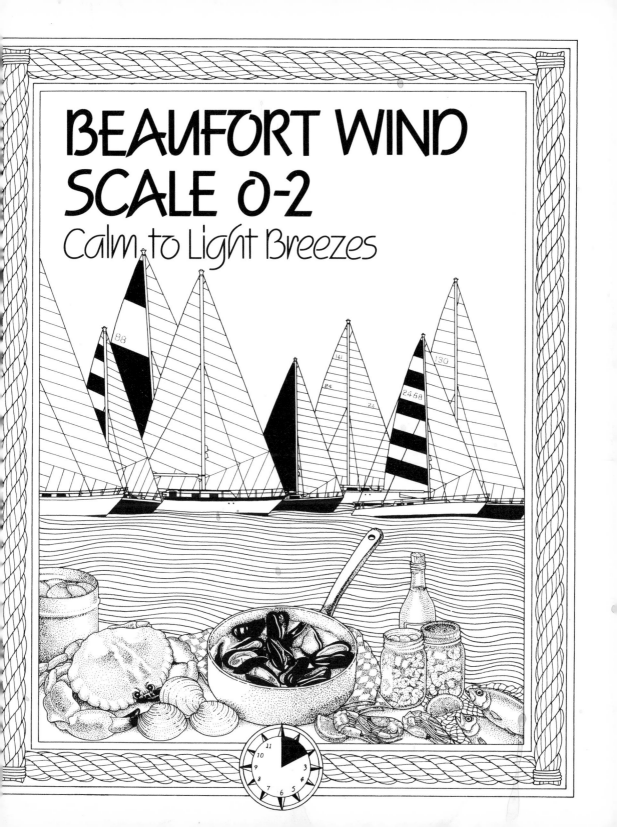

BEAUFORT WIND SCALE 0-2
Calm to Light Breezes

SANDWICH FILLINGS

French-type loaves split and filled with an assortment of spreads, fish and meat are an excellent sandwich to take on a day's sail or perhaps when racing around the buoys. Start filling the loaf at one end with some scrambled egg, then perhaps salami followed by egg mayonnaise or some pâté, tomatoes, peanut butter and so on until you run out of loaf. Wrap the sandwich in aluminium foil or Cling Film until needed and cut off a slice for each person. They can then nibble their way down the sandwich, peeling off the wrapping as they go. There are an enormous variety of fillings to suit all tastes. Here are some of my family's favourites.

Cottage Cheese and Dates

110 g (4 oz) plain cottage cheese   55 g (2 oz) stoned dates

Chop the dates into small dice and mix together with the cottage cheese.

Curried Scrambled Egg

15 g (½ oz) butter or margarine   2 eggs, lightly beaten
1 teaspoon curry paste   salt and pepper

Melt the butter in a small pan over a low heat, add the curry paste and fry gently for about 2 minutes. Add the eggs and a little salt and pepper. Stir from time to time until the eggs are creamy and soft. Remove from the pan just before the eggs look fully set.

Egg Mayonnaise

1 hard-boiled egg   black pepper
1 tablespoon ready-made
   mayonnaise

Cut up the egg, add the mayonnaise and seasoning and mix well.

Cold Mackerel

55 g (2 oz) leftover cold   1 teaspoon horseradish sauce
   mackerel   15 g (½ oz) butter

Mash together all the ingredients in a bowl to make a smooth pâté.

Carrots and Raisins

30 g (1 oz) raisins
boiling water

1 large carrot, grated
a little vinegrette dressing

Put the raisins in a bowl and pour over enough boiling water to cover. Leave to soak for 30 minutes. Mix together the carrot and vinegrette dressing. Drain the raisins and add to the carrot mixture.

Salmon Pâté

200 g (7 oz) tin of salmon,
   drained
1 teaspoon dried dill
1 tablespoon mayonnaise

5 cm (2 in) cucumber, very
   finely chopped
salt and pepper

Put the drained salmon into a bowl and carefully remove any bones or skin. Add the dill, mayonnaise and cucumber and mix well with a fork. Season well.

Bully Pâté

55 g (2 oz) bully beef
1–2 teaspoons strong mustard
1 tablespoon mayonnaise

Mash together all the ingredients in a bowl.

MELON AND TOMATO COCKTAIL

Nicolas Parsons, quizmaster of 'Sale of the Century'

SERVES 6

1 honeydew melon
3 large ripe tomatoes, peeled
3 ripe bananas
a little lemon juice, fresh
   or bottled
EITHER 300 ml ready-made
   mayonnaise OR:
1 large egg
1 egg yolk

pinch of dry mustard
pinch of caster sugar
salt and pepper
300 ml (½ pint) vegetable oil
1 dessertspoon white wine
   vinegar
1 dessertspoon freshly chopped
   mixed herbs *or* 1 teaspoon
   mixed dried herbs

Though not strictly necessary, if possible make the mayonnaise the day before it is required as the flavour improves with keeping. To make the mayonnaise by hand: put the egg yolk, mustard, sugar, salt and a little pepper in a small bowl and beat well together. Very slowly, drip the oil in a little at a time, stirring constantly. As the mayonnaise starts to thicken, it is possible to add the oil a little more quickly. When the emulsion is really thick, beat in the vinegar to thin the consistency. Stir in the herbs, check the seasoning and store in a cool place until needed.

To make the mayonnaise in a food processor: use the cutting blade. Put the egg, egg yolk and seasonings in the bowl. Switch on, mix together for a few seconds, then pour in the oil slowly. When all the oil has been added, pour in the vinegar to thin the consistency. Switch off and check the seasoning. Store in a cool place until needed.

To make the cocktail: slice the top off the melon about a quarter of the way down. Trim the ends of both pieces so that they will stand upright. Using a teaspoon or a melon ball cutter remove the pips and scoop the flesh of the melon into balls. Peel the tomatoes by plunging them into a bowl of boiling water for 1 minute, then drain and peel off the skins. Cut the tomatoes in eighths and remove the pips. Peel and chop the bananas and sprinkle them with lemon juice. Mix together all the fruit and pile into the larger half of the melon. Pour the mayonnaise into the 'lid' and serve immediately.

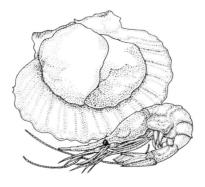

CARROT AND ORANGE SOUP

Peter and Joan Phillips   *TRAVACREST SEAWAY,* ex-*LIVERY DOLE III*

Peter Phillips is a West Country ex-copper who has helped raise money for children's charities over the years and who also lives life to the hilt, taking up any challenge that comes his way from scrambling to single-handed sailing. He is one of Britain's most popular and enthusiastic multi-hull sailors.

SERVES 4

450 g (1 lb) carrots, peeled and diced	300 ml (½ pint) chicken stock
30 g (1 oz) butter	300 ml (½ pint) milk
1 small onion, finely chopped	a little salt
1 dessertspoon cornflour	black pepper
grated rind and juice of half an orange	2 tablespoons double cream or natural yoghurt

Melt the butter in a saucepan, add the carrots and onion and cook gently for about 5 minutes, or until the onion is soft but not browned. Stir in the cornflour and grated orange rind and gradually add the orange juice, stock and milk. Bring to the boil, reduce the heat, cover and simmer for about 20 minutes or until the carrots are very tender. Remove from the heat, allow to cool for a few minutes, then pass the soup through a sieve or purée in a liquidizer or food processor. Check the seasoning and, just before serving, stir in the double cream or yoghurt. This soup is equally delicious served hot or cold.

GNOCCHI PARISIENNE

Her Grace Lavinia, Duchess of Norfolk

Her Grace is the vice-patron of the Jubilee Sailing Trust. This is one of her favourite dishes, quite delicious but one which, she says, few people seem to make really well. The only difficult part of the recipe is in the poaching, that is, not allowing the water to boil too fast. The water should be barely moving or the gnocchi will fall to pieces. Every time you cut a length from the nozzle, use a knife dipped in hot water which will stop the paste from sticking to your fingers.

SERVES 4

200 ml (⅓ pint) milk
110 g (4 oz) butter
170 g (6 oz) plain flour
4 medium eggs
140 g (5 oz) grated Gruyère
   ***or* Emmenthal cheese**

1 teaspoon French mustard
salt and pepper
For the sauce:
300 ml (½ pint) Mornay sauce
   (see page 71)

Put the milk and butter together in a saucepan and bring to the boil. Remove from the heat, add the flour and beat until smooth and the mixture starts to leave the side of the pan. Allow to cool and then add the eggs one at a time, beating well with each addition. Mix in 110 g (4 oz) of the grated cheese, the mustard and seasoning.

Turn the mixture into a forcing bag with a plain nozzle. (If a forcing bag is not available, drop small pieces of the mixture into the water from a teaspoon.) Fill a large frying pan with water to within 14 mm (½ in) of the top, bring to the boil and reduce the heat until the water is barely moving. Pipe 2.5 cm (1 in) lengths of the paste into the water using a knife dipped in hot water to cut it. Poach for about 10–12 minutes or until firm. Remove with a slotted spoon.

Arrange in one layer in a buttered, ovenproof dish. Coat with a Mornay sauce, sprinkle with the remainder of the grated cheese and bake in a preheated moderate oven (180°C/350°F, gas mark 4) for 20 minutes, or until the top is golden. Serve immediately with a salad, if serving it as a main course.

MACKEREL GRAVAD LAX

Peter and Patricia Trumper   *MISTRESS MINE*

This traditional Scandinavian dish of raw marinated salmon has become a familiar item on many menus. Salmon, however, is in the luxury class for most people but the humble mackerel and the much abused farm trout marinated like this almost defy description.

SERVES 4

2 large mackerel
2–3 sprigs of fresh fennel
70 g (2½ oz) rock or sea salt
140 g (5 oz) Demerara sugar
4 tablespoons of chopped fresh
    dill *or* 2 tablespoons dried
    dill
2 dessertspoons chopped fresh
    thyme *or* 1 teaspoon dried
    thyme
2 dessertspoons chopped fresh
    oregano *or* 2 teaspoons
    dried oregano

small sprig of chopped fresh
    rosemary *or* 2 teaspoons
    dried rosemary
For the sauce:
2 tablespoons natural thick
    yoghurt
2 tablespoons French mustard
1 dessertspoon sugar
1 tablespoon fresh dill chopped
    or 2 teaspoons dried dill
1 tablespoon lemon juice, fresh
    or bottled

Clean, bone and fillet each fish as described on page 24.

Put the fennel on the bottom of a shallow dish and then lay two fillets, skin side down, on top of it. Mix together thoroughly the salt and sugar in a small bowl and spread half of this mixture on top of the fillets. Sprinkle over half of the chopped or dried herbs. Place the other two fillets on top, skin side down. Spread the remaining salt mixture and herbs on top.

Cover the fish with first greaseproof paper and then foil and place a heavy weight on top of the fillets. Refrigerate for a minimum of 24 hours. To make the sauce, stir all the ingredients into the yoghurt and mix well. Serve with rye bread, a dollop of sauce and a wedge of lemon on each plate.

POTTED SHRIMPS

Peter de Savary   *VICTORY 83*

Peter's favourite way to start a meal on board his yacht is potted shrimps. Made at home and frozen in individual tubs they can be turned out and decorated with freshly chopped parsley and a slice of lemon.

SERVES 4

225 g (8 oz) prepared shrimps
110 g (4 oz) unsalted butter
pinch of cayenne pepper

juice of half a lemon *or*
    1 tablespoon bottled lemon juice
black pepper

Prepare the shrimps: peel fresh and thaw frozen ones.

Melt one tablespoon of the butter in a saucepan and when foaming add the shrimps, cayenne, lemon juice and black pepper. Heat gently together, stirring constantly, until the shrimps are heated through but not browned. Do not allow the mixture to boil. Divide the fish and butter mixture between four individual tubs or ramekin dishes.

Melt the remainder of the butter over a high heat and when it is foaming skim off the surface, leaving the sediment at the bottom. Pour over the shrimps and make sure they are well covered. Leave until the butter is firm, then cover and freeze. Bring them to room temperature before turning out of their pots and serving with brown toast or buttered brown bread and butter.

STUFFED MUSSELS

It is more usual to serve mussels prepared this way in their half shells, swimming in the garlic butter. However, due to lack of space on board (unless you have a very large grill) it is easier to pick them out of their shells and serve them straight from the grill pan.

SERVES 4

40 large mussels, cleaned and scrubbed	1 small onion, very finely chopped
60 ml (2 fl oz) white wine	2–3 cloves garlic, crushed
170 g (6 oz) butter	2 tablespoons freshly chopped parsley
	55 g (2 oz) fresh breadcrumbs

Prepare the mussels as described on page 27, discarding any that refuse to shut. Put the mussels in a large saucepan and add the wine. Cover the pan and cook on a moderate heat, shaking the pan from time to time so that all the mussels come into contact with the heat. Cook for about 6–10 minutes or until all the mussels are open. Drain the mussels in a colander and remove them from their shells, discarding any that remain shut. Arrange the mussels in the grill pan.

Mix together the butter, onion, garlic and parsley in a bowl and dot the mussels with this mixture. Cook under a preheated hot grill until the butter begins to melt. Remove from the heat, shake the pan to make sure the mussels are evenly coated in the butter and sprinkle with the breadcrumbs. Return to the heat and cook until the top is golden brown. Serve while still sizzling hot.

MOULES À LA MARINIÈRE

There are many variations of this classic dish. Here is a simple version.

SERVES 6

1.8 kg (4 lb) mussels, cleaned and
   scrubbed
30 g (1 oz) butter or margarine
1 large onion, finely chopped
2 cloves garlic, finely chopped
1 bay leaf

150 ml (¼ pint) dry white wine
2 tablespoons freshly chopped
   parsley
black pepper
2 tablespoons single cream *or* top
   of the milk

Prepare the mussels as described on page 27, discarding any that refuse to shut. Melt the butter in a large saucepan, add the onion and garlic and fry gently until it is soft, but not browned. Add the mussels, bay leaf and white wine. Cover the pan and cook on a moderate heat for about 6–10 minutes, or until all the mussels are open. Shake the pan from time to time so that all the mussels come into contact with the heat. Drain into a colander, reserving the liquid. Discard any mussels that remain shut.

   Put the mussels into a large serving bowl and carefully strain the liquid back into the pan. Add the parsley, season with pepper and cook on a high heat until the liquid has reduced. Remove from the heat and stir in the cream or top of the milk and then pour over the mussels. Serve with crusty French bread and a chilled white wine.

STUFFED CLAMS

Peter and Patricia Trumper   *MISTRESS MINE*

These large clams can be bought from the Helford River.

SERVES 4

16 clams, cleaned and scrubbed
a little cold water
170 g (6 oz) butter
2–3 cloves garlic, crushed

2 tablespoons freshly chopped
   parsley
55 g (2 oz) fresh breadcrumbs

Prepare the clams as described on page 25. Put one layer of clams in a large saucepan and add a little water. Cook on a moderate heat and the moment the clams open, remove at once and replace with an unopened clam. Do not allow the clams to boil or they will become extremely tough. Drain and remove the top shell of each clam.

Mix together the butter, garlic and parsley in a bowl. Arrange the clams in the grill pan and spread the garlic butter on top of each clam. Sprinkle with the breadcrumbs. Cook under a preheated hot grill until the butter has melted and the top is a golden brown. Serve immediately with some crusty bread and a good white wine.

FISH CAKES

Suzi Scneideman   *DIVIRTIMENTI*

This recipe for fish cakes is slightly different from most in that the fish cakes are best served cold with mayonnaise. They bear no relationship to those orange-coloured and tasteless horrors so often passed off as the real thing. Prepare them at home to take down to the boat for the weekend and eat either hot or cold for breakfast. They must be eaten within 24 hours of preparation.

MAKES 12

450 g (1 lb) cod fillet *or* any
   firm-fleshed fish such as
   haddock or hake
1 small onion, finely chopped
2 tablespoons freshly chopped
   parsley

1 tablespoon plain flour
1 egg, lightly beaten
1 blade of mace, crumbled
salt and pepper

oil for frying

Wash the fish, remove the skin and carefully pick out any bones left on the flesh. Either pass the fish through a mincer with the onion or chop both very finely. Mix together the fish, onion, parsley, flour, egg and mace in a bowl until smooth, season well and beat again.

Shape into 12 golfball-sized pieces and then flatten them slightly with the palm of your hand. Heat about 7 mm (¼ in) of oil in a frying pan and when sizzling gently slide the fishcakes into the pan, baste each one with a spoonful of oil and fry for 2 minutes on either side. Remove and drain on kitchen paper.

Serve warm with a tomato sauce or cold with mayonnaise flavoured with lemon and capers or Tabasco and a little tomato purée.

PILCHARD QUICHE

Martin Muncaster   *COTTONTAIL*

Martin is a well-known broadcaster at the BBC. He says that his wife makes this quiche at home to take down to the boat as a lunch or supper dish. It is equally tasty eaten hot or cold.

SERVES 6–8

225 g (8 oz) plain or wholemeal
   flour
½ teaspoon salt
110 g (4 oz) butter or
   margarine
1 tablespoon cold water
For the filling:
425 g (15 oz) tin of pilchards
   in tomato sauce

3 medium eggs, lightly beaten
salt and pepper
150 ml (¼ pint) single cream or
   top of the milk
plenty of freshly chopped
   parsley

Sift the flour and salt into a large bowl. Cut the butter or margarine into dice and rub into the flour mixture, using your fingertips, until the mixture resembles fine breadcrumbs. Sprinkle the water over the flour mixture. Mix lightly together, adding a little more water if necessary to make a firm dough.

If you are using a food processor, sift the flour and salt into the bowl with the knife in place. Cut the butter or margarine into dice. The fat should have come straight from the fridge or freezer. Tip into the bowl and switch on the processor at high speed for a few seconds, or until the mixture resembles fine breadcrumbs. With the mixer still running, carefully add the water a teaspoon at a time, until the dough begins to ball on the knife. Press the dough lightly into a ball, wrap it in greaseproof paper and refrigerate for at least 30 minutes.

Roll out the pastry thinly on a lightly floured surface. Butter a 30-cm (12-in) in diameter pie tin. Lift it carefully on the rolling pin and lay it gently over the tin. Ease the pastry into shape, without stretching it, and trim the edges.

Weight it with dried beans and bake in a preheated moderately hot oven (200°C/400°F, gas mark 6) for 15 minutes.

While the case is baking, prepare the filling. Mash the pilchards in a bowl with a fork, add the beaten eggs, cream and parsley and mix well. Add the salt and pepper to taste. Remove the pastry case from the oven, spoon the pilchard mixture into it and spread evenly. Dust the top with black pepper and return the quiche to the oven and bake at 180°C/350°F, gas mark 5 for about 20 minutes or until the filling has set and the top is a golden brown.

CORNISH PASTY

Daphne du Maurier   *JEAN D'ARC*

Daphne du Maurier says that Cornish pasties were a particular favourite when she was younger with both her and her husband, General Browning. Their boat was moored on some still waters, usually in a creek on some Cornish river. Daphne recommends that you prepare all the ingredients before going down to the boat and then assemble the pasty on board.

MAKES 4

450 g (1 lb) shortcrust pastry   2 large potatoes, diced
  (see page 39)   110 g (4 oz) turnip, diced
1 egg yolk   2 large onions, finely chopped
a little milk   55 g (2 oz) butter
For the filling: salt and pepper
450 g (1 lb) lean beef steak

Divide the pastry into 4 portions. Roll out each portion on a lightly-floured surface and cut out 4 circles about the size of a large tea plate of 18-cm (7-in) in diameter.

Trim the meat of excess fat and chop it finely. Mix together the potatoes, turnip and onions in a bowl along with the butter. Season well. Divide the filling equally and place in the centre of each pastry circle. Dampen the edges of the pastry and draw the two opposite sides together over the filling. Press the edges together firmly over the top of the pastry. Crimp the sealed edge with your fingers. Put on a baking tray and brush with a little beaten egg yolk and milk.

Bake in a preheated hot oven (220°C/425°F, gas mark 7) for 20 minutes. Then reduce the heat to moderately hot (200°C/400°F, gas mark 6) and bake for a further 40 minutes. Serve hot or cold with a chilled beer.

Eila Rose Sea Food Mornay

Edward Bourne   *EILA ROSE*

Edward is the secretary of the Royal Cruising Club. He explained to me how this dish was originally created. One year, while cruising along the Norwegian coast, discovering that he and his crew could not really afford restaurant prices, they decided instead to create a truly gastronomic meal. They waited until after dark and then took the rubber dinghy and a powerful torch and propelled the dinghy silently around the precarious rocks of the fjord. They shone the torch down to about two inches below the water level where large crabs were clearly visible. With the aid of the torch and bare hands they hoisted the crabs into the dinghy. Wisely, they had taken the precautions of wearing shoes and taking a puncture repair kit with them.

Next morning, before the sun got too hot, they set off to the nearby rocks and removed as many mussels as they thought they needed. Next, the crew's resident botanist was sent off into the hills with instructions not to return until she had found wild garlic, sorrel and strawberries. Finally, after fashioning a shrimping net out of a redundant pair of tights and some stiff wire, they caught plenty of shrimps in the shallows.

A white sauce was next prepared, into which was grated the rinds of a truckle of Cheddar brought from home. The boiled and picked-over crabs, mussels and shrimps were thrown into the sauce along with six hard-boiled eggs. This was put into the oven and a fantastic meal was had by all.

Here is a simple version of the same meal even if you don't happen to be in Norway:

SERVES 4

170 g (6 oz) prepared crab meat	*For the sauce:*
170 g (6 oz) mussels, cooked and removed from their shells	15 g (½ oz) butter
	15 g (½ oz) plain flour
170 g (6 oz) shrimps, peeled	300 ml (½ pint) milk
4 hard-boiled eggs, halved	45 g (1½ oz) grated Gruyère, Emmenthal,
30 g (1 oz) grated cheese	Parmesan *or* Cheddar cheese

Prepare the crab, mussels and shrimps as described on pages 25–28 and pile into an ovenproof dish with the hard-boiled eggs.

Melt the butter in a small saucepan and stir in the flour. Cook the *roux* for a minute or two and, away from the heat, gradually add the milk, stirring constantly. Return to the heat and bring to the boil, then reduce the heat and simmer for 2–3 minutes. Add the grated cheese and cook gently for a further 5 minutes. Pour the sauce over the seafood and eggs and sprinkle with the remainder of the grated cheese. Cook in a preheated hot oven (200°C/400°F, gas mark 6) for about 20 minutes to heat through. Quickly brown the top under a preheated hot grill. Serve with a green salad and a bottle of crisp, dry white wine, preferably a Chablis or a Pouilly-Fumé.

SQUID IN RED WINE

Liz Hammick   *WRESTLER OF LEIGH*

This recipe is redolent of the Mediterranean, conjuring up memories of warm summer evenings. Squid are not difficult to prepare and are well worth the little effort involved. As this is a robust and rich dish, make sure that your crew have their sealegs before serving them this while under way.

SERVES 4

450 g (1 lb) squid, cut into rings	½ teaspoon freshly chopped or
2 tablespoons olive oil	dried basil
2 medium onions, thinly sliced	½ teaspoon sugar
2 cloves garlic, crushed	salt and pepper
425 g (15 oz) tin of tomatoes	freshly chopped parsley and
120 ml (4 fl oz) red wine approx.	black or green olives to
1 tablespoon tomato purée	garnish

Prepare the squid as described on page 28. Heat the oil in a large saucepan, add the onions and garlic and fry gently for about 5–6 minutes until the onion is soft, but not browned. Add the squid and fry for a further 3–4 minutes. Stir in the tomatoes and their juice, red wine, tomato purée, basil and sugar and mix well. Cover the pan and simmer gently for about 30 minutes, or until the squid are tender.

Remove as many of the squid as possible with a slotted spoon and keep warm. Increase the heat and boil rapidly until the liquid has reduced as the sauce should not be too thin. Check the seasoning and add a little more sugar if necessary. Return the squid to the pan and sprinkle with freshly chopped parsley and a few olives. Serve immediately with plenty of fresh bread or plain, boiled rice and a salad.

BAHAMIAN GRILLED FISH

'Spud' Spedding

Spud learnt this method of cooking fish from Captain Franklin Clarke who skippered *Victory*'s tender during the 1983 America's Cup. Although the recipe calls for red snapper, Spud assures me that it is equally delicious using bass, mullet or even the humble mackerel.

SERVES 4

2 red mullet, bass or mackerel	55 g (2 oz) coarse salt
30 g (1 oz) red and green chillies,	1–2 tablespoons fresh lime
deseeded and finely chopped	juice
1–2 cloves garlic, peeled and	
chopped	

Clean, bone and fillet each fish as described on page 24. Mix together the chillies, garlic and salt with enough of the lime juice to make a paste. Spread the paste evenly and thinly over the fillets and place under a preheated hot grill. Grill for 10–12 minutes, turning them once after the first side is browned. The skin should be golden brown. Serve immediately and wash down with copious amounts of very cold beer!

MACKEREL BAKED WITH GOOSEBERRIES

Peter and Patricia Trumper   *MISTRESS MINE*

SERVES 4

4 small mackerel
2 tablespoons fresh tarragon,
   chopped *or* 1 dessertspoon
   dried tarragon
2–3 sprigs of chopped fresh
   thyme *or* 1 teaspoon dried thyme
110 g (4 oz) fresh breadcrumbs

400 g (14 oz) tin of gooseberries,
   drained
salt and pepper
300 ml (½ pint) dry cider,
   dry white wine *or* elderflower
   wine

Clean and gut the fish as described on page 24, removing the head, tail and backbone. Mix together the herbs, breadcrumbs and gooseberries in a bowl and season well. Fill the mackerel with this mixture and press back into shape. Arrange the fish in an ovenproof dish and pour over the cider or wine.

   Cover and bake in a preheated moderately hot oven (200°C/400°F, gas mark 6) for 20–30 minutes. Serve immediately with plain, boiled potatoes and a salad.

SMOKED MACKEREL BAKE

Peter and Patricia Trumper   *MISTRESS MINE*

SERVES 2

2 smoked mackerel fillets
4 large tomatoes, sliced *or* 400 g
   (14 oz) tin of tomatoes, drained
55 g (2 oz) grated Gruyère *or*
   Cheddar cheese

2 tablespoons single cream *or*
   top of the milk
55 g (2 oz) fresh breadcrumbs
30 g (1 oz) butter

Remove the skin of the fish and carefully pick out any bones left on the flesh. Break up the flesh into large flakes and cover the base of a buttered ovenproof dish with some of the fish. Top with tomatoes and cheese, then dribble over some of the cream. Repeat layers finishing with the remaining cream.

Cover with the breadcrumbs, dot with the butter and bake in a preheated moderately hot oven (200°C/400°F, gas mark 6) for 30 minutes, or until golden brown and sizzling. Serve immediately with some crusty French bread and a green salad.

FRICASSÉE OF CHICKEN

Dame Mary Donaldson   *ROGGER*

Dame Mary Donaldson was Lord Mayor of London in 1983–84. Apart from being a very keen supporter of the Jubilee Sailing Trust, she is an enthusiastic sailor.

SERVES 4

1 1.6 kg (3½ lb) chicken	110 g (4 oz) plain flour
140 g (5 oz) butter or margarine	4 large carrots, cut into
1 small onion, chopped	7 mm (¼ in) slices
600 ml (1 pint) dry white wine	450 g (1 lb) mushrooms, quartered
600 ml (1 pint) chicken stock	150 ml (¼ pint) double cream

Joint the chicken into eight pieces, allowing two pieces per person. Melt 30 g (1 oz) or 2 tablespoons of the butter or margarine in a large pan, add the chicken pieces and lightly brown them on all sides. Lift them out and arrange in a flameproof casserole. Melt the remaining butter in the pan, add the onion and cook gently for a few minutes until the onion is soft, but not browned. Measure the wine and the stock into another pan and bring quickly to the boil. Remove from the heat as soon as it boils.

Sprinkle the onions with the flour, mix well and scrape up all the juices in the pan. Gradually add the hot wine and stock and bring to the boil slowly, stirring constantly. Reduce the heat and simmer for about 5 minutes. Add the carrots and mushrooms to the sauce and then pour over the chicken in the casserole. Cover the casserole and place in a preheated moderate oven (160°C/325°F, gas mark 3) for an hour, or until the chicken is tender. Check the seasoning, allow to cool and refrigerate. Reheat to serve on top of the stove, add the cream but do not allow to boil. Serve with plain, boiled rice and a salad. This dish should be eaten within 48 hours of the initial preparation.

CHICKEN CURRY

Chay Blyth   *BEEFEATER II*

Chay has made many heroic voyages from rowing across the Atlantic with John Ridgeway to sailing Round the World alone against the prevailing winds. Chay says that he doesn't do much cooking while racing and relies on packet curries. This is his favourite recipe that his wife, Maureen, makes for him to take sailing.

SERVES 4

4–8 chicken pieces
cold water to cover
85 g (3 oz) butter
1 large onion, sliced
1 clove garlic, crushed
425 ml (¾ pint) chicken stock
1½ teaspoons ground coriander
  seeds
1½ teaspoons ground cumin seeds
1 teaspoon ground chillis
1 teaspoon ground cardamon *or*
  4 whole cardamon pods, crushed

½ teaspoon fenugreek
½ teaspoon ground mixed spice
½ teaspoon ground turmeric *or*
  yellow food colouring
1 green pepper, deseeded and
  sliced
1 potato, peeled and diced
4 cm (1½ in) stick of cinnamon,
  crumbled
1 bay leaf

Put the chicken pieces into a pan and add enough cold water to cover. Bring to the boil, then reduce the heat and simmer for about 30 minutes. Strain, reserving the stock. You can either flake the flesh from the bones or leave the pieces whole. Mix together the spices, apart from the cinnamon, in a bowl. Melt the butter in a pan, add the onion, garlic and mixed spices and fry gently for a few minutes, or until the onion is soft. Add the chicken pieces and fry until browned on all sides.

Make up the leftover stock from the chicken to 600 ml (1 pint). Add the stock, green pepper and potato, bay leaf and crumbled cinnamon stick to the pan. Bring to the boil then reduce the heat, cover and simmer gently for 30 minutes. If a thicker curry is preferred add a little cornflour slackened with water. Just before serving, fish out the cinnamon stick and bay leaf and serve with fried rice, poppadums, Bombay Duck and hot mango kasundi.

CARBONNADE OF BEEF

Cheaper cuts of meat are greatly improved by marinating. Not only does it help to tenderize the meat, but it also enhances the flavour.

SERVES 4–6

900 g (2 lb) stewing steak	1 dessertspoon plain flour
4 juniper berries, crushed	300 ml (½ pint) water or beef stock
2 medium onions, sliced	pinch of mixed dried herbs
2 large carrots, roughly chopped	1 tablespoon brown sugar
600 ml (1 pint) brown ale	1 teaspoon French mustard
seasoned flour	salt and pepper
1 tablespoon oil	2 tablespoons double cream
30 g (1 oz) butter	(optional)

Trim the meat and cut into large cubes. Put the meat, juniper berries, onions and carrots into a plastic food container and pour over the brown ale. Cover with a lid and marinate overnight. Remove the meat from the marinade with a slotted spoon and dry the meat on kitchen paper. Reserve the liquid and vegetables. Dip the meat in the seasoned flour. Heat half of the oil and butter together in a large saucepan, add the meat and brown it quickly on all sides. Lift out the meat and set aside.

Reduce the heat, add the onions, and brown them evenly without allowing them to burn. Remove and set aside. Melt the remaining oil and butter, add the flour and cook the *roux* on a gentle heat for a few minutes until it turns nut brown. Gradually stir in the marinade liquid and the stock, and bring to the boil slowly stirring constantly, to make a thick, smooth sauce. Add the herbs, sugar, mustard and seasoning and simmer for a further 1 or 2 minutes. Arrange the meat, onions and carrots in a heavy casserole and pour over the sauce which should just cover the meat, if not add a little more water. Cover the casserole tightly and cook in a preheated moderate oven (160°C/325°F, gas mark 3) for 2½–3 hours, or until the meat is very tender. Check the seasoning and stir in the cream, if you are using it, but do not let it boil.

Pressure cooker version: To adapt the above recipe, use the pressure cooker to fry the meat and onions but make the sauce in another pan. Pour the sauce over the meat, onions and carrots making sure the sauce covers the meat, if not add a little more water. Cook, according to the manufacturer's instructions, on high pressure for 20 minutes.

SIAMSA HOT POT

Winki and Georgina Nixon   *TURTLE*

Winki and Georgina Nixon sent me this recipe which comes from some of their sailing friends.

Siamsa (Irish for shamrock and pronounced 'shamsha') is a Ruffian 33 which is cruised extensively to all the islands around the Celtic fringe by the venerable threesome of Micky d'Alton, Franz Winklemann and Leslie Latham whose average age is somewhat above the statutory retirement level. However, despite this and the small size of their boat, they cruise in style and comfort – quite some achievement as Franz is so tall that he has to be jack-knifed to go below! Their Siamsa Hot Pot is simple to prepare and full of robust flavours. Micky d'Alton considers that its greatest advantage is that it is made entirely from fresh ingredients which keep well at sea.

I am not too sure that Irish rashers of bacon are the same as English bacon. Unsmoked gammon cut is probably closer to the original as it is not very fatty or cut too thinly. Using sea water is perfectly all right as long as you are sailing in a reasonably unpolluted area!

SERVES 3

450–680 g (1–1½ lb) new potatoes, scrubbed

2–3 large onions, peeled and cut in half

450–680 g (1–1½ lb) Irish rashers, *or* unsmoked gammon, sliced

300 ml (½ pint) sea water

Arrange the scrubbed potatoes at the bottom of a heavy, large saucepan. Put the onions on top and cover with the bacon rashers. Pour over the sea water – there should be at least 5 cm (2 in) in the saucepan – and cover tightly. Bring to the boil, then reduce the heat and simmer gently for 20–30 minutes, or until the potatoes are just tender.

SHEPHERD'S PIE

Peter de Savary   *VICTORY 83*

Having started his meal with potted shrimps (see page 35), Peter's favourite main course is shepherd's pie accompanied by two freshly-cooked green vegetables. This is also an ideal dish for preparing at home, freezing and then taking down to the boat.

SERVES 4

450 g (1 lb) lean minced beef	**Worcestershire sauce** *or*
1 tablespoon dripping	**mushroom ketchup**
2 medium onions, finely chopped	**salt and pepper**
2 medium carrots, finely chopped	*For the topping:*
1 tablespoon plain flour	**450 g (1 lb) potatoes**
300 ml (½ pint) good beef stock	**30 g (1 oz) butter**
110 g (4 oz) mushrooms, roughly	**a little milk**
chopped	**salt and pepper**
tomato ketchup	

Heat the dripping in a large saucepan and when foaming add the minced beef and fry quickly until it is evenly browned. Remove the meat with a slotted spoon and keep warm. Add the onions and carrots to the fat in the pan and cook gently until they are soft, but not browned. Sprinkle the onions and carrots with the flour, stir well and allow it to colour. Gradually stir in the stock, tomato ketchup and Worcestershire sauce. Bring to the boil and then reduce the heat, add the mushrooms and simmer gently for about 5 minutes. Return the meat to the pan, check the seasoning and pour the mixture into a buttered ovenproof dish. Leave in a cool place until cold.

Peel and cut up the potatoes. Cover with cold salted water and bring up to the boil. Cook quickly until the potatoes are tender – about 20 minutes – then drain and mash them well. Season well with salt and pepper, add the butter and a little milk and beat well with a wooden spoon until they are creamy and smooth. When the meat mixture is cold, spoon the potato topping over the meat and, using a fork, spread evenly.

Cook in a preheated moderately hot oven (200°C/400°F, gas mark 6) for 45 minutes. Cool quickly, cover with aluminium foil and freeze.

To cook from frozen: place in a preheated moderately hot oven (190°C/375°F, gas mark 5) for 1 hour and remove the foil 20 minutes before the end of the cooking time to allow the top to brown. If the pie has been thawed, just remove the foil and cook in a preheated hot oven (200°C/400°F, gas mark 6) for 30 minutes.

MEXICAN VEAL STEW

Sue Lloyd-Evans   *THICKET*

SERVES 4–6

900 g (2 lb) stewing veal
2 tablespoons oil
30 g (1 oz) butter
2 medium onions, chopped
1 tablespoon cornflour
1 dessertspoon paprika
1 tablespoon tomato purée

600 ml (1 pint) chicken
  stock
200 g (7 oz) tin of sweetcorn,
  drained
200 g (7 oz) tin of red
  pimentoes, drained and cut
  into strips

Cut the veal into cubes and trim off any excess fat. Heat the oil and butter together in a saucepan, add the meat and brown it quickly on all sides. Remove the meat with a slotted spoon and set aside. Reduce the heat, add the onions and fry until golden brown but without allowing them to burn. Remove the pan from the heat and sprinkle the onions with the flour, paprika and tomato purée.

Gradually stir in the stock and bring to the boil slowly, stirring constantly, to make a thick, smooth sauce. Check the seasoning and return the meat to the pan. Transfer the stew to a flameproof casserole, cover tightly and cook in a preheated moderate oven (180°C/350°F, gas mark 4) for about 2 hours, or until the meat is tender. Add the tins of sweetcorn and pimentoes and simmer for a further 10–15 minutes. Serve immediately with plain, boiled rice.
Pressure cooker version: To adapt the above recipe, prepare the stew as above but do not add the flour, slackened with a little water, until the end. After adding the stock, cook according to the manufacturer's instructions, on high pressure for 20 minutes. Release the steam slowly, add the tins of sweetcorn and pimentoes and check the seasoning. If the meat is tender simmer for a further 10 minutes without the lid, but if the meat is not quite tender bring to pressure again and cook for a further 6 minutes. Add the flour, slackened with a little water, to the stew to thicken.

DEVILLED PORK FILLET

Sue Lloyd-Evans *THICKET*

SERVES 6

900 g (2 lb) pork fillet
30 g (1 oz) oil
30 g (1 oz) butter
2 medium onions, roughly
  chopped
1 large green pepper, deseeded
  and sliced
225 g (8 oz) mushrooms, sliced or
  left whole if small

30 g (1 oz) plain flour
2 teaspoons strong French
  mustard
2 dessertspoons Worcestershire
  sauce
2 tablespoons tomato ketchup
1 tablespoon brown sugar
600 ml (1 pint) chicken or light
  stock

Heat the oil and butter together in a large saucepan until it foams. Trim away any fat, skin and sinew on the outside of the pork fillet. Cut the pork into 14 mm (½ in) slices and fry quickly in the oil until lightly browned on both sides. Remove with a slotted spoon and set aside. Reduce the heat and add the onions, pepper and mushrooms and fry for a few minutes until the onions are soft, but without allowing them to burn. Remove with a slotted spoon and reserve with the meat.

Stir the flour into the remaining fat in the pan and cook the *roux* on a gentle heat for a minute or two until it turns nut brown. Gradually add the stock, stirring constantly, to make a smooth sauce. Stir in the mustard, Worcestershire sauce, tomato ketchup and sugar. Bring to the boil and return the meat and vegetables to the pan. Check the seasoning. Either simmer the stew on a very low heat or transfer to a flameproof casserole with a well-fitting lid and cook in a preheated moderate oven (160°C/325°F, gas mark 3) for about an hour, or until the meat is tender. Serve immediately with plain, boiled rice.

SARIE MARAIS STEW

David Gay *SARIE MARAIS*

David is the offshore commander of the Sea Cadet Corps. When he is not sailing *Royalist* he is usually sailing his own boat, *Sarie Marais*. This is the stew that he reckons he has got down to a fine art over the years and which is much appreciated by his hungry crews during the cool, typical British summer weather.

SERVES 5–6

30 g (1 oz) butter or margarine
4 large onions, sliced
1 tablespoon flour
300 ml (½ pint) good beef
stock
2 450 g (1 lb) tins of stewing
steak
225 g (8 oz) tin of peas, drained

450 g (1 lb) tin of potatoes,
drained
200 g (7 oz) tin of oxtail soup
200 ml (⅓ pint) red wine
pinch of dried mixed herbs
grated cheese or Parmesan

Melt the butter or margarine in a large saucepan, add the onions and fry until they are well browned and crisp. Remove them with a slotted spoon and drain on kitchen paper. Keep them warm. Stir the flour into the fat in the saucepan and gradually add the stock, bringing to the boil slowly. Add the tinned ingredients, the wine and herbs. Reduce the heat and simmer for about 20 minutes. If the stew looks too watery, thicken it by adding about a tablespoon of dehydrated potato powder. Serve in deep bowls and sprinkle over the fried onions and grated cheese or Parmesan.

WOBBLY ROAST LAMB

Winki and Georgina Nixon   *TURTLE*

Winki and Georgina sent me the following instructions for preparing a superb roast dinner on board: 'Take one joint of best Wicklow Hills lamb (from the hills of Wicklow, Ireland but English lamb or perhaps Welsh will do) and stow carefully in an obscure and supposedly cool corner of a rather primitively-equipped 30-foot sloop. (We have no fridge or freezer and reckon that an ice box is usually more trouble than it's worth.) Forget all about having this meat on board until strongly reminded after a couple of days through the functioning of the olfactory organ. Wash it (the meat not the olfactory organ) in the cockpit with the best wine vinegar until the pong is reasonably eliminated. Stuff with as much garlic and whole black peppercorns as possible. Place in a fairly hot oven and retire to the pub if reasonably adjacent.'

'During this phase of roasting, it is the duty of the youngest crew member to return regularly to the boat to check that all is well. If agreement cannot be reached as to who is the youngest, this is the skipper's task. After two or three pints, cook returns to the vessel to oversee the final stages of roasting and cook best new potatoes (with mint), cauliflower and carrots in the pressure cooker.'

'Rest of the crew return on board after three or four pints (in total) to consume meal in reverent silence, washed down with white wine which has been chilled by prior suspension on seabed from line knotted with enormous care. Dinner to be eaten with much smacking of the lips for the gratification of the cook. Dishes to be washed in due course by everyone except the cook. Then return to the pub and breathe heavily over everyone in the snug until space is cleared for crew to be comfortably ensconced for a review of the meal.'

SERVES 4–6

2.3 kg (5 lb) leg or shoulder of lamb

3–4 cloves garlic, peeled and thinly sliced
8 black peppercorns

Make several incisions into the lamb with the point of a sharp knife. Cut the garlic into thin slices and, using your fingertips, insert the slivers of garlic and peppercorns into the meat. Put the joint of meat in a roasting tin and roast in a preheated moderately hot oven (190°C/375°F, gas mark 5) for about 1½–2 hours, basting the meat frequently.

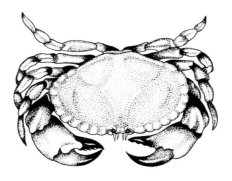

ROSSINI LAMB CHOPS

Not quite the authentic version perhaps, but the closest you can achieve on board with the minimum of fuss and without breaking the bank! It is an ideal supper dish to be eaten in some delightful anchorage after a visit to the pub – and the butcher.

SERVES 4

4 lamb chops
55 g (2 oz) butter
110 g (4 oz) tin of liver pâté with truffles
110 g (4 oz) mushrooms, finely sliced

1 clove garlic, crushed
1 tablespoon orange juice
2 tablespoons sweet sherry (if sweet is unavailable, dry will do)
a little black pepper

Melt the butter in a large frying pan, add the chops and fry over a moderate heat for about 4–5 minutes on either side. The time they will take to cook will depend on their thickness but they should just be pink in the middle. Remove the chops from the pan, spread each with a generous teaspoon of the pâté and keep them warm.

Wipe the mushrooms with a damp cloth and slice the caps and stalks finely. Add the mushrooms and garlic to the pan, turning them constantly until their juices begin to run. Add the orange juice, sherry and the remainder of the pâté to the pan, stirring constantly for a further few minutes. Divide the sauce equally between the chops and serve immediately with plain, boiled rice.

DG'S CURRY

Peter Thompson

Peter Thompson is the Director General of the Jubilee Sailing Trust and he says that he should not be held responsible should anyone singe their mouths while eating this curry.

SERVES 4

3–4 tablespoons olive oil
100 g (3½ oz) butter

½–1 teaspoon ground hot red chillis or to taste

1 teaspoon poppy seeds
4 medium onions, roughly
  chopped
3–4 cloves garlic, chopped
450 g (1 lb) stewing steak,
  shoulder or leg of lamb *or*
  chicken cubed
2 dessertspoons ground turmeric
1 teaspoon ground coriander seeds
1 teaspoon ground cardamon or
  4 whole cardamon pods,
  crushed

8 whole cloves or 1 teaspoon
  ground cloves
1 teaspoon ground ginger *or*
  small piece fresh green ginger,
  peeled and coarsely chopped
450 g (1 lb) tin of tomatoes
600 ml (1 pint) light or chicken
  stock
salt and pepper
2 dessertspoons desiccated
  coconut
4 hard-boiled eggs, halved

Heat together the oil and butter in a large saucepan and add the poppy seeds. After a few minutes they will begin to 'pop'. Reduce the heat, add the onions and garlic and fry until the onions are soft, but not browned. Remove the onions with a slotted spoon and keep warm. Increase the heat, add the trimmed cubes of meat and lightly brown them on all sides. Reduce the heat again and return the onions to the pan with the turmeric. If you are using whole spices crush them in a pestle and mortar. Add the ground or crushed spices to the meat, mix well and cook gently for a few minutes.

Stir in the tomatoes and their juice and enough stock to cover the meat and season well. Bring to the boil, stirring constantly, then cover, reduce the heat and simmer gently for 1–1½ hours, or until the meat is tender. (Beef will take longer than chicken.)

When the meat is quite tender, leave the curry to cool for at least 6 hours before eating to absorb the full flavour of the spices. Just before serving reheat the curry to just below boiling point, check the seasoning and add the coconut and hard-boiled eggs. Serve with plain, boiled rice.

ARRIVING CURRIES

Libby Purves   *BARNACLE GOOSE*

Libby is a well-known journalist and broadcaster who needs no further introduction from me! She says: 'we always have an arriving curry to mark the end of a notable passage on board *Barnacle Goose.* You can add almost any tinned or packet stuff to one of these provided that you have real onions, curry powder and various garnishes such as dried banana, apple, coconut flakes and chutney. Therefore we always keep a curry bag, containing these essentials, and hide it away from nightwatch feasts along the way! If there are any curry remains the next day, they are turned into a fine mulligatawny soup through the addition of a tin of tomato soup.'

Here then is Libby's recipe:

SERVES 4

2 tablespoons oil
2 medium onions, chopped
2 cloves garlic, chopped
1–2 tablespoons curry powder
   or paste
425 g (15 oz) tin of stewed steak,
   meatballs or chicken in white
   sauce

425 g (15 oz) tin of baked beans
200 g (7 oz) tin of mixed
   vegetables
a little potato powder (optional)
salt and pepper
dried banana, apple and coconut
   flakes

Heat the oil in a large frying pan, add the onions and garlic and cook on a low heat until the onions are soft, but not browned. Stir in the curry powder or paste and sauté very gently for about 5 minutes. Add the contents of all the tins, bring to the boil, season and then simmer over a low heat for about 20 minutes or until the curry is heated through. If the curry looks a little too thin, thicken by adding a little dehydrated potato powder. Just before serving sprinkle over the banana, apple and coconut flakes. Serve with boiled rice.

PRE-COOKED BAKED POTATOES

Richard and Maura Fanshawe   *ZERLINA*

Richard and Maura say that if shops can do it, then so can you!

SERVES 4

2 large potatoes
30 g (1 oz) butter

110 g (4 oz) grated cheese
cayenne pepper

Scrub the potatoes well, prick with a fork and bake in a preheated moderately hot oven (200°C/400°F, gas mark 6) for 1–1¼ hours, according to their size.

Mix together the grated cheese, butter and cayenne pepper in a bowl. Cut the potatoes in half lengthwise and make 2–3 diagonal crosses each way across the cut halves. Pile the cheese mixture on top, pressing down firmly.

To reheat, place on a baking tray and bake in a preheated hot oven (200°C/400°F, gas mark 6) for about 20 minutes or until sizzling hot and golden brown on top.

Glynn Christian is the Breakfast Time food reporter and chef. He is also an intrepid explorer and has made expeditions to Pitcairn Island. He contributed the following nine recipes to the book.

WARM WATERCRESS, POTATO AND BACON SALAD

Watercress is native to both Europe and Western Asia and it has been cultivated further afield with great success. Although sometimes too great: in the waterways of my own native New Zealand, it is a serious weed hazard. It needs a continual supply of running water to grow in and commercially this means springs and boreholes for maximum purity as river-grown watercress may carry typhoid or other diseases. Hampshire is Britain's watercress capital and one company there grows a quarter of the country's entire consumption. Use it when it is as dark and as fresh as possible.

SERVES 4

450 g (1 lb) small new potatoes
  or 450 g (1 lb) tin of new
  potatoes, drained
225 g (8 oz) streaky bacon

2 bunches of watercress
2 tablespoons sunflower oil
2 tablespoons wine vinegar

If you are using fresh potatoes, scrub the potatoes clean, place in cold salted water, bring to the boil and cook until tender, about 15–20 minutes. Drain at once and leave until cold enough to handle, then slice lengthwise. If you are using tinned potatoes, drain and slice them lengthwise.

Slice the bacon, leaving the rind on, into 2.5 cm (1 in) lengths. Put the bacon, without additional fat, into a non-stick frying pan and cook on a low heat until the fat runs and the bacon is crisp.

Wash the watercress, removing any coarse stalks and shake dry. Divide the watercress into four even helpings, arrange on large plates and top with the potato slices. Remove the bacon from the pan with a slotted spoon and sprinkle it over the leaves. Add the oil and the vinegar to the hot bacon fat in the pan, bring to the boil scraping up all the juices and bits in the pan and then spoon over the salads.

ORANGE MUSHROOMS

Since mushrooms first began to be commercially cultivated on a large scale in the late 1940s, they have become enormously popular and rightly so. But don't forget that mushrooms aren't always button-sized; these are immature mushrooms and if they were to stay where they were they would eventually grow into big mushrooms, commercially known as 'opens' or 'flats'. These, for my money, have much more flavour than the little ones and I think it is much nicer to enjoy them on their own, as a starter, rather than forever slicing them into a sauce at the last minute. Here are two versions, one without the customary butter and one with.

SERVES 2–3

Slimmers' version:

450 g (1 lb) large open mushrooms
3 tablespoons fresh orange juice
1½ tablespoons lemon juice,
   fresh or bottled

30 g (1 oz) freshly chopped parsley
1 clove garlic, freshly chopped
   (optional)
salt and pepper

Wipe the mushrooms, trim the stalks and slice thickly. Put them in a non-stick pan and cook them over a moderate heat, moving and turning them constantly with a wooden spoon to prevent them from sticking or burning, rather like Chinese stir-frying. When the juices of the mushrooms start to run, add the orange and lemon juice. When this sauce starts to bubble, stir in the parsley and cook for a further 30 seconds, stirring constantly. Remove from the heat and add the garlic if you are using it. Check the seasoning and serve immediately with unbuttered bread to soak up the juices.

Gourmands' version:

450 g (1 lb) large open mushrooms	**4 tablespoons fresh orange juice**
2 cloves garlic, finely chopped (optional)	**2 tablespoons lemon juice, fresh or bottled**
110 g (4 oz) butter	**30 g (1 oz) freshly chopped parsley**

Wipe the mushrooms, trim the stalks and either leave the mushrooms whole or quarter them, whichever you prefer. Chop the stalks finely with the garlic, if you are using it (and it is good). Melt the butter in a frying pan and gently fry the mushrooms for 3 minutes on each side. Add the chopped garlic and stalks and fry for a further 1½ minutes. Increase the heat and add the orange and lemon juice. Slowly let the sauce bubble to give the mushrooms some of the flavour. Add the parsley and mix well. Serve each mushroom or mushroom quarter with the sauce poured over and bread which will need no butter as it soaks up all the juices.

CHICKEN WITH MINTED AVOCADO

This was the first, and still one of the most requested, recipes I created for the first year of *Breakfast Time*.

SERVES 4

1 1.35–1.6 (3–3½ lb) chicken	**30 g (1 oz) butter or margarine**
1 large bunch of fresh mint leaves	**1 ripe avocado pear**
juice and peel of 1 lemon	**150 ml (¼ pint) double cream**

On a flat surface lay out enough aluminium foil to wrap around the chicken. Place the chicken in the centre and put the mint inside and underneath the chicken. Pour the lemon juice over the chicken and put the peeled rind inside. Rub the butter over the chicken and wrap up the foil loosely, leaving room for steam. Cook in a preheated moderate oven (180°C/350°F, gas mark 4) for 1¼ to 1½ hours, or until tender.

Cut the avocado in half lengthwise. Twist to loosen the stone and separate. Remove the stone and pull off the skin, leaving as much of the bright green layer on the flesh as possible.

When the chicken is tender, remove from the oven and strain the juices into a small pan. Stir in the cream, then add the avocado slices and heat gently for about 5 minutes. You need heat the avocado through only – not cook it. Cut the chicken into 4 pieces and pour over the sauce, arrange the avocado slices as garnish with a sprinkling of grated lemon peel or some fresh mint leaves. Serve with new, boiled potatoes or noodles.

PARSLEY-SMOTHERED LIVER AND BACON

Nothing is more nutritious than liver and nothing can be as delicious. Yet the occasional piece with an off-taste makes many lovers of liver more wary than they need be – me included. In this recipe the old trick of soaking liver in milk avoids that and also makes cheaper liver – including pigs' liver – very acceptable. By cutting the bacon up you can also get a more even blend of flavours and avoid the problem of overcooking the one in order to avoid undercooking the other. If you really cannot do without onions, then use some in this recipe but I think you'll prefer the liver without this intrusion.

SERVES 4

450 g (1 lb) lambs' liver	black pepper
enough milk to cover the liver	½ teaspoon salt
225 g (8 oz) lean back bacon	150 ml (¼ pint) sherry, *or* white or
2–3 cloves garlic, chopped	red wine *or* vermouth
(optional)	55 g (2 oz) freshly chopped parsley
2 dessertspoons plain flour	

Trim and thinly slice the liver and place in a shallow dish. Add milk to cover and leave to soak for at least 2 hours or overnight if more convenient. Drain the liver well and discard the milk.

Cut the bacon into 5 cm (2 in) strips discarding the rind and put the bacon, without additional fat, into a frying pan. Cook over a low heat until the fat runs and the bacon is crisp. Add the garlic, if you are using it, but do not let it colour too much. Remove the bacon and garlic with a slotted spoon, put it onto a warm serving plate and keep warm. Mix together the flour, salt and pepper on a plate and dip both sides of the liver in it. Put the liver into the remaining fat in the pan and cook slowly until it is as pink or as well done as you like – between 5 and 10 minutes – depending also on how thick the liver is. Lift out the liver and add it to the bacon and garlic.

Pour the alcohol into the pan and boil the liquid rapidly for 1 minute, scraping up all the pan juices and bits to flavour the sauce. Add the parsley, bring back to the boil and pour the sauce over the liver and bacon. Serve immediately with a salad and, to make the meal more substantial, some very creamy and smooth mashed potato.

PECULIARLY GOOD OXTAIL

Although classic oxtail soups and stews are delicious, they're not terribly popular fare these days. There seem to be two reasons for this: firstly they are rich food and make rather heavy eating. Secondly, they are high in fat and this worries more and more cooks nowadays. I've created the following recipe with these problems in mind. The recipe's two outstanding features are the use of celery, a magically successful partner for oxtail and the use of beer and tomatoes which, with their natural acids, give a more even taste and prettier look to the final dish – so now you can unlock your past without imperilling your future.

SERVES 6

2 oxtails	790 g (1 lb 12 oz) tin of tomatoes
8 tablespoons olive oil	or 2 400 lb (14 oz) tins,
seasoned flour	drained
4 sticks of celery, cut into	2 bay leaves
2.5 cm (1 in) lengths	6 cloves garlic, peeled and left
600 ml (1 pint) bitter	whole

Trim the oxtails of excess fat and cut into 5 cm (2 in) lengths. Heat half of the olive oil in a heavy frying pan. Dip the oxtail into the seasoned flour and fry until it is well browned. Remove the oxtail with a slotted spoon and set aside. Discard any burnt oil or flour remaining in the pan. Heat the remainder of the oil in the same pan, add the celery, and cook it gently until it begins to soften slightly. Pour over the best bitter and bring it to the boil, stirring constantly, scraping up all the juices and bits in the pan.

Arrange the oxtails, tomatoes, bay leaves and garlic in a flameproof casserole and pour over the liquid and celery. The liquid should just cover the oxtails. Bring to the boil on top of the stove, then cover tightly and cook very slowly for 3–4 hours, or until the oxtail easily comes away from the bone. Fish out the bay leaves at the end of the cooking time.

Pressure cooker version: To adapt the above recipe, prepare the oxtail as above. After adding the liquid to the pan, cook, according to the manufacturer's instructions, on high pressure for 40 minutes. At the end of the cooking time, leave it to cool and then skim off the fat that has settled on the surface.

HELLO SAILOR BREAD AND BUTTER PUDDING

Although bananas have been grown commercially for about 3,000 years they did not arrive in this country until the sixteenth century. Perhaps one of the reasons why more recipes don't exist for them in British cookery is that they were a real luxury item until the Imperial Direct Line started shipping them from the West Indies in 1901. Few people realize, by the way, that the banana plant, some 30 feet high, is not botanically a tree but one of the world's largest herbs!

SERVES 4–6

6–8 slices of white bread	2 medium eggs
30 g (1 oz) butter	600 ml (1 pint) milk
2–3 teaspoons ground cinnamon	6 tablespoons dark rum
1 very ripe banana	3 tablespoons sugar, brown or
55 g (2 oz) raisins *or* sultanas	white
grated rind and juice of 1 lime	

Choose almost any white bread other than a sliced sandwich loaf as this will become a nasty mush. Butter the bread lavishly and discard the crusts. Sprinkle with cinnamon and cut into thin strips. Peel and slice the banana and mix together in a small bowl with the dried fruit, rind and juice of the lime. Cover the bottom of a buttered overproof dish with bread and butter strips and then sprinkle over the banana mixture. Repeat layers finishing with a layer of bread and butter.

Crack the eggs into another bowl and lightly beat in the milk, rum and sugar. Pour the custard over the bread and butter mixture and leave the pie to soak for about 30 minutes, pushing the top layer under the liquid from time to time until all the liquid is absorbed. Bake in a preheated moderate oven (180°C/350°F, gas mark 4) for about 40–50 minutes, or until the custard is set and the top is golden brown. Serve when the pudding is warm with a generous helping of whipped cream to which you have added another tablespoon of dark rum.

BLACK CHERRY OVEN PANCAKE

Nothing beats this recipe for a spectacular but simple pudding. It's really a small Yorkshire Pudding so be sure that the oven and baking dish are as sizzling hot as possible.

SERVES 4

For the batter:
85 g (3 oz) plain flour
2 eggs
150 ml (¼ pint milk)
For the sauce:
450 g (1 lb) tin of black cherries,
  drained and juice reserved

4 tablespoons butter
3 dessertspoons soft brown sugar
3 dessertspoons black rum *or*
  brandy

Sift the flour into a bowl and make a well in the centre. Add the eggs and, using a wooden spoon, mix from the centre, gradually drawing in the flour from the outer edges. Stir in the milk, beating well until the batter is smooth and thick. Drain the cherries, reserving the juice, and put into a 25-cm (10-in) pie dish with the butter and sugar. Place in a preheated very hot oven (240°C/475°F, gas mark 9) until it is very hot and bubbling. Take out and quickly add the batter and bake for a further 15 minutes. Meanwhile put the reserved juice from the cherries and rum or brandy in a small pan and cook on a high heat until the syrup has reduced by at least a half. When the pancake is well risen and golden brown take out of the oven and serve in wedges with the hot cherry, syrup and rum poured over. Serve with fresh whipped cream, if available, and perhaps a little more rum!

PINEAPPLE AND MINCEMEAT PIE

First mention of pineapples in Britain, native to South America, was made after they were presented to Oliver Cromwell and yet they were afterwards regarded as a great delicacy by Charles II. Palates before politics! Their wonderful shape is formed by the tiny fruits of all their flowers gradually fusing into one. You will often see the shape used decoratively as the pineapple was regarded as a symbol of hospitality during the great country house era.

SERVES 4–6

450 g (1 lb) shortcrust pastry (see page 39)
For the filling:
1 fresh pineapple *or* 680 g (1½ lb) tin of pineapple rings or chunks in natural juice, drained

55 g (2 oz) Demerara sugar
225 g (8 oz) jar of good mincemeat
½ teaspoon ground ginger

If using fresh pineapple, remove the skin and slice the flesh into chunks. If using tinned pineapple, drain and cut into chunks. Sprinkle with the Demerara sugar.

Divide the pastry into two and roll out one piece slightly larger than a buttered 20–23 cm (8–9 in) pie dish. Line the dish with the pastry. Spoon the mincemeat into the pastry case and arrange the pineapple on top. Sprinkle with the ginger. Roll out the remaining pastry to a circle large enough to cover the pie. Dampen the pastry rim and cover the pie with the pastry top. Press round the edges to seal and decorate the pie with any cuttings. Bake in a preheated moderately hot oven (200°C/400°F, gas mark 6) for 10 minutes, then reduce the temperature to cool (150°C/300°F, gas mark 2) and bake for a further 20 minutes.

THE TRIFLE

Surprisingly there is no basic traditional recipe for a trifle. It was originally a pudding made up of layers and covered with jellies, creams and custards. Mrs Beeton regularly gave recipes for what she called an Indian trifle and which involved cutting cold rice flour into shapes and piling them into an elaborate tower smothered and stuffed with as many colourful ingredients as you or your cook could get your hands upon. Other versions were topped with high whips, an extravagant type of syllabub.

Since Mrs Beeton's time almost universal agreement has been reached as to what ingredients a trifle should comprise. It should be a layered affair and served in a glass bowl. The bottom layer should consist of sponge squares, split and generously smeared with strawberry or raspberry jam. (A sliced jam roll suits very well.) The sponge is sprinkled lavishly with a sweet sherry or port – dry sherry simply does not work. In Australia and New Zealand the sponges are often held together with a flavoured jelly instead of using alcohol and this is also a good idea when cooking for children.

The next layer traditionally is a fruit one and it is a pity it is usually tinned fruit salad. Any fresh fruit would be better – even orange segments – but tropical delights such as kiwi fruit, mango and passion fruit taste the best if you cannot get hold of soft summer fruits. The custard comes next and, to many, only custard made with powder tastes right. That is hard to refute! Yet egg custard would be more authentic if you could make it well. Flavour it liberally with the old-fashioned favourites such as coconut, orange flower water, grated rind and so on. Lastly, whipped cream is the inescapable topping, often studded with toasted almonds and cherries.

Now, once you know that almost anything layered can quite properly be called a trifle, there is no need to stick to the basic recipe at all. The proportion of any one layer to another is absolutely up to you which is why I have decided not to be dogmatic and write out a recipe. Here are a few interesting ideas:

- layer the sponges with lemon or orange curd (from a jar), dribble on sherry, brandy or calvados, use stewed apple (from a tin) flavoured with orange or lemon and top with citrus-flavoured custard
- use apricot or peach jam (particularly if you happen to be sailing in France as their jam is extremely good), brandy, sherry, or apricot brandy, fresh peaches or apricots sprinkled with toasted hazelnuts and an almond- or brandy-flavoured custard
- spread the sponges with crushed blackberries, sprinkle with gin or brandy, layer with stewed apples or more soft summer fruits and top with a raspberry or blackberry syllabub
- use cherry jam, fresh cherries and rum or cherry brandy; tinned crushed pineapple, lime juice and gin or rum; or use chocolate sponge, fresh

raspberries, brandy and cream flavoured with rosewater. In fact, use anything you like provided it is fresh, good quality, colourful and seasonal

- trifle is best served the next day so don't add the cream until the last minute. If it is made long in advance then it is able to exchange flavours. Finally, make sure you serve it really cold.

CHOCOLATE MOUSSE

Her Grace Lavinia, Duchess of Norfolk

This is the most delicious chocolate mousse and definitely for eating after you've finished sailing for the day! It also freezes extremely well.

SERVES 8–10

4 eggs, separated
85 g (3 oz) caster *or* granulated sugar
170 g (6 oz) drinking chocolate
150 ml (¼ pint) milk

350 ml (12 fl oz) double cream
1–2 tablespoons kirsch (optional)
2 teaspoons powdered gelatine, dissolved in 2 tablespoons cold water

Separate the eggs, placing the yolks in one bowl and the whites together in a second bowl. Add the sugar to the yolks and over a pan of barely simmering water beat the eggs until they are light and fluffy.

Put the chocolate in another pan with the milk and slowly bring to the boil, stirring constantly, and simmer gently until the mixture is smooth. Set the mixture aside to cool slightly and then add it to the egg yolks, mixing well. Stand the bowl in a sink of cold water or on top of some ice cubes to allow the mixture to become quite cold. Meanwhile, measure the 2 tablespoons of cold water into a small saucepan and sprinkle in the gelatine. Allow to soak for 5 minutes, then stir over a low heat, without boiling, to dissolve the gelatine. Add the gelatine to the chocolate mixture, pouring it in a thin, steady stream. Leave the mixture in a cold place until it is just beginning to set.

Whip the double cream until it holds soft peaks and then fold it carefully into the chocolate mixture with the kirsch, if you are using it. Whisk the egg whites until they hold stiff peaks and fold them into the chocolate mixture. Pour into a serving or soufflé dish and chill until set. Before serving, sprinkle over some crumbled flaky chocolate to decorate.

CORTOLA

Jock McLeod   *MOONRAKER*

In 1962–63 Jock McLeod sailed to Brazil with Peter and Ann Pye and this is the Brazilian sweet they enjoyed on their first meal ashore at Recife after their passage from the Cape Verde Islands.

SERVES 4

4 slices of bread
55 g (2 oz) butter
4 bananas
55 g (2 oz) Gruyère, Emmenthal *or*
   Cheddar cheese, sliced

55 g (2 oz) sugar
1 teaspoon ground cinnamon to taste

Lightly toast the bread on each side. Melt the butter in a large frying pan. Peel the bananas and cut in half lengthwise, add to the hot butter in the frying pan and fry until they are lightly browned on both sides. Remove the bananas from the pan, put two halves on each piece of toast and cover evenly with the cheese.

Place under a preheated hot grill until the cheese has melted and is beginning to bubble. Remove from the grill and sprinkle generously with the sugar mixed with cinnamon. Serve immediately while the toast, bananas and cheese are still hot and the sugar is quite cold.

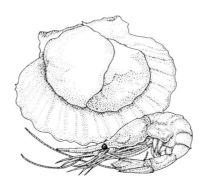

BANANAS FLAMBÉ

During the 1982 two-handed Round Britain and Ireland Race, I had to phone into a radio station and report how we were getting on, what the weather was doing and also what we were eating. The galley was very limited so describing what we were eating was the hardest part of the broadcast, especially during the rough weather we experienced along the west coast of Ireland. However, I broadcast the following recipe much to the amusement of several other crews who were listening in. We didn't eat this until we were safely at anchor in Castlebay.

SERVES 2

30 g (1 oz) butter	2 ripe bananas
3 tablespoons dark brown sugar	2–3 tablespoons dark rum

Melt the butter and sugar in a large frying pan. Peel the bananas and cut in half lengthwise. Add to the hot butter and sugar in the pan and fry until lightly browned on both sides. Remove the pan from the heat and add the rum. Tip the pan over the flame to ignite it and reheat gently, shaking the pan so that the flames spread over the entire contents. Turn off the heat and swirl the pan round until the flame is extinguished. Serve immediately with the liquid spooned from the pan and, if available, with fresh cream.

TYFOON SCONES

Gustave Versluys   *TYFOON VI*

Gustave is a delightful Belgian who regularly takes part in long-distance, single-handed events. He was awarded the much-coveted Outstanding Seamanship prize in the 1981–82 Whitbread Round the World Race. He is a professional boatbuilder and is currently building a new boat for the 1985 Round the World.

As a slight variation you can omit the sugar and stir in a 110 g (4 oz) tin of creamed sweetcorn to make sweetcorn fritters. Fry in a little melted butter or half butter and half oil.

MAKES 8–10

55 g (2 oz) plain flour	**a little milk**
1 teaspoon sugar	
2 large eggs	**oil for frying**

Sift the flour and sugar into a large bowl, make a hollow in the centre of the flour mixture and crack in the eggs. Using a wooden spoon, stir thoroughly from the centre of the bowl, drawing in the flour from the outer edges. Add a little milk if necessary to make a thick and smooth batter.

Place a heavy frying pan over a moderate heat and rub with a little oil. When the pan is really hot, drop tablespoons of the mixture, spaced well apart, into the pan. Cook the scones for about 3 minutes on each side. They are best eaten with jam, honey or even cheese. As the batter will keep for a day, cook some scones at breakfast and cook the remainder of the mixture for tea.

PRETZELS

Laurel Holland

450 ml (¾ pint) warm water	**450 g (1 lb) sharp Cheddar cheese,**
1 tablespoon sugar	**grated**
15 g (½ oz) dry yeast	**1 egg, lightly beaten**
680 g (1½ lb) plain flour	**coarse salt (optional)**
1 teaspoon salt	

Heat the water to lukewarm (about 40°C/104°F) and add the sugar and yeast. Leave in a warm place for about 5 minutes to froth.

In a large bowl mix the flour, salt and grated cheese and pour in the yeast mixture. Mix to a stiff dough and add a little extra flour if necessary. Knead the dough on a lightly-floured surface for about 5–10 minutes, or until it is smooth and supple. Break off walnut-sized pieces of dough and roll them between your hands, shaping them into either the traditional pretzel shape, loops or initials.

Put the pretzels on an ungreased baking tray and leave them to double in size in a warm place for about an hour, depending on the temperature. Brush the tops of the pretzels with the egg and sprinkle with the coarse salt, if you are using it. Bake in a preheated hot oven (220°C/425°F, gas mark 7) for about 15–18 minutes, or until well risen and golden brown.

CREAMY TOMATO SAUCE

This is a very quick and easy tomato sauce that can be used as an accompaniment to a savoury soufflé, such as cheese or tuna, or as a sauce for pasta, hamburgers or a cottage pie.

SERVES 2–4

15 g (½ oz) butter or margarine
15 g (½ oz) plain flour
450 g (1 lb) tin of tomatoes
½ teaspoon sugar
1–2 cloves garlic, crushed
1 bay leaf

pinch of basil *or* 1 dessertspoon
   pesto sauce
salt and pepper
1–2 tablespoons single cream
   (optional)

Melt the butter in a pan and stir in the flour. Remove from the heat and add the juice from the tin of tomatoes, stirring constantly, to make a thick and smooth sauce. Return to the heat and add the tomatoes, breaking them up with a fork or spoon. Add the sugar, garlic, bay leaf, basil or pesto sauce, season well and simmer gently for about 10 minutes, stirring from time to time. A tablespoon or two of cream can be added just before serving to make it extra special. Fish out the bay leaf before serving.

BARBEQUE SAUCE

This piquant sauce keeps for at least two to three weeks in a fridge and probably for as long on board without a fridge provided it is kept in a cool place. It is ideal for accompanying chops, sausages, hamburgers and spare ribs as well as cold meat. It can be served hot or cold and adds a completely different character when smothered over a shoulder of lamb or pork halfway through the cooking time.

SERVES 6–8

1 tablespoon oil
15 g (½ oz) butter
1 large onion, finely chopped
6 tablespoons tomato purée
4 tablespoons Worcestershire sauce

4 tablespoons wine vinegar
4 tablespoons Demerara sugar
150 ml (¼ pint) chicken stock

Heat the oil and butter together in a pan and add the onion. Cook gently for a few minutes until the onion is soft, but not coloured. Add the remainder of the ingredients and bring up to the boil, stirring well. Cover, reduce the heat and simmer for about 10 minutes. If the sauce looks too thick, add a little more stock or water. Serve hot or cold.

MORNAY SAUCE

This classic sauce goes particularly well with vegetables, eggs, poached fish and chicken. Here are some serving suggestions: add a little wine and a clove of crushed garlic, pour it over eggs on a bed of spinach and bake in the oven; flavour it with some strong mustard and a little dry cider and serve it with grilled mackerel; or add a little white wine and about 150 ml (¼ pint) of single cream to accompany chicken.

MAKES 300 ml (½ pint)

1 small onion stuck with 2 whole cloves	300 ml (½ pint) milk
	30 g (1 oz) butter
1 small carrot	30 g (1 oz) plain flour
1 bay leaf	55 g (2 oz) grated cheese
4 peppercorns	salt and pepper

Put the onion, carrot, bay leaf and peppercorns in a small pan with the milk and bring to the boil. Simmer for about 30 minutes and then strain into a jug.

Melt the butter in a saucepan and stir in the flour. Cook the *roux* for a minute or two, gradually add the strained milk, stirring constantly, and bring to the boil to make a thick and creamy sauce. Reduce the heat and simmer gently for a further 5 minutes. Add the grated cheese, then season to taste with salt and pepper.

CAROLINE'S BITS

Sir Peter and Lady Johnson   *INNOVATION*

No name has been found for this regular crew fodder other than Lady Johnson's (Caroline's) bits.

MAKES ABOUT 30

110 g (4 oz) butter or margarine	110 g (4 oz) sultanas (optional)
2 tablespoons golden syrup	225 g (8 oz) Rich Tea or digestive
1 tablespoon drinking chocolate	biscuits

In a small saucepan melt together the butter, golden syrup and drinking chocolate on a low heat. Mix in the sultanas if you are using them. Crush the biscuits to crumbs and, using a fork, stir into the butter mixture.

Press this mixture firmly into a well-buttered 28 × 18 cm (11 × 7 in) shallow baking tin and leave to set in a cool place until quite cold and set firm. Cut into about 30 squares and store in an airtight tin. Leave the tin near the companionway at night for easy access in all weather!

A TODDY FOR A COLD NIGHT IN HARBOUR
(but only if you are not putting to sea until the next day)

Colin and Rosemary Mudie

Colin is a naval architect and has designed many famous boats including: *Royalist*; the *Brendan* (used on Tim Severin's epic voyage across the Atlantic); and the *Lord Nelson*, the Jubilee Sailing Trust's sailing vessel.

Rosemary and Colin warn you to be wary of this drink as it can have a quite remarkable effect and people have been known to start singing surprisingly bawdy songs after a couple of glasses.

FOR EACH SERVING

1 measure of Pernod
2 measures blackcurrant syrup
hot water to taste

Put one-third of Pernod to two-thirds blackcurrant syrup into a tumbler and top up with hot water to taste. Stir and serve.

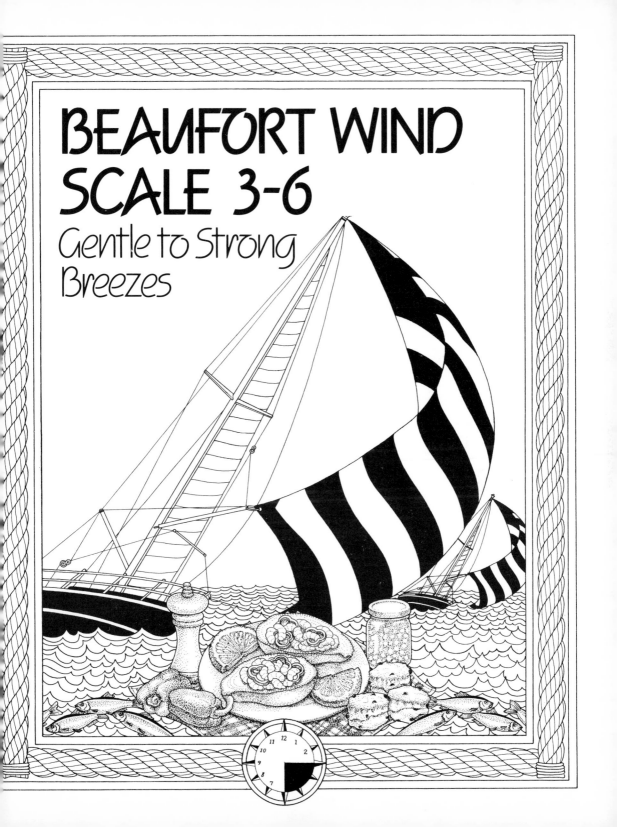

BEAUFORT WIND SCALE 3-6

Gentle to Strong Breezes

LENTIL SOUP

Priscilla Gamble   *BRIGAND CHIEF*

A thick soup.

SERVES 4

225 g (8 oz) orange lentils
1 tablespoon oil
2 rashers smoked streaky bacon,
   diced
1 large onion, sliced
1 large carrot, peeled and diced
2 sticks of celery, chopped *or*
   425 g (15 oz) tin of celery
1 medium potato, peeled and
   grated

pinch of dried thyme
1 bay leaf
1.2 litres (2 pints) chicken or light
   stock
salt
lemon juice, fresh or bottled,
   to taste

Heat the oil in a large saucepan, add the diced bacon and cook on a gentle heat until the fat runs and the bacon is crisp. Add the onion and cook until the onion begins to brown, but without allowing it to burn. Stir in the lentils, carrot, celery, potato, thyme, bay leaf and stock. If you are using a tin of celery then pour in its juice as well.

Bring to the boil, stirring constantly, then reduce the heat, cover and simmer gently for about 45 minutes, or until the lentils are quite soft. Check the seasoning and add a little lemon juice to taste. Fish out the bay leaf and serve immediately.

THICK MUSSEL SOUP

If the mussels come from a sandy place make sure that you rinse them in several changes of water. This is a thick and hearty soup, filling and nutritious.

SERVES 2

900 g (2 lb) mussels, cleaned and
   scrubbed
1 small onion, finely sliced

1–2 cloves garlic, finely chopped
300 ml (½ pint) pale ale
30 g (1 oz) butter

15 g (½ oz) plain flour
150 ml (¼ pint) milk
small strip lemon rind

200 g (7 oz) tin of butter beans, drained
salt and pepper
freshly chopped parsley

Prepare the mussels as described on page 27. Put the mussels in a large saucepan with the onion and garlic. Pour over half of the lager, cover the pan and cook on a moderate heat for about 6–10 minutes, or until the mussels are open. Shake the pan from time to time so that all the mussels come into contact with the heat. Drain into a colander, reserving the liquid. Discard any mussels that remain shut.

Melt the butter in the saucepan and stir in the flour. Cook the *roux* for a minute or two, then draw aside from the heat and gradually add the mussel liquid, the remainder of the ale and the milk. Return to the heat and bring to the boil, stirring constantly to make a thick, smooth sauce. Reduce the heat, cover and simmer for 10 minutes, adding a little more milk if necessary and the lemon rind. Pick the mussels from their shells and add to the soup with the butter beans. Check the seasoning and, just before serving, sprinkle with the freshly chopped parsley.

ONION SOUP

Desmond Hampton   *WILD RIVAL*

Desmond describes himself as a very reluctant chef and says that this soup was created more by accident than through experience!

SERVES 1

2 large onions, sliced
30 g (1 oz) butter
1 large potato, peeled and sliced
1 litre (1¾ pints) beef stock
salt and pepper

1 bay leaf
1 thick slice of toast
1 clove garlic, peeled and left
    whole
30 g (1 oz) grated cheese

Melt the butter in a large saucepan, add the onions and fry gently until the onions are golden brown, without allowing them to burn. Add the potato and fry for a further 10 minutes. Stir in the stock and bring to the boil. Season well and add the bay leaf. Reduce the heat and simmer gently for at least 30 minutes.

Rub the toast with the garlic, cover with the grated cheese and put in the bottom of a deep bowl. Fish out the bay leaf. Pour over the soup and eat with a spoon and fork.

CHICKEN SOUP WITH DUMPLINGS

SERVES 4

1 chicken carcass
2 litres (3½ pints) water
2 medium onions
3 whole cloves
4 sticks celery *or* 425 g (15 oz) tin
   of celery
4 black peppercorns

3 medium carrots
juice of ½ a lemon
2 strips of lemon rind, very finely
   chopped
salt and pepper
8 dumplings (see page 93)

Put the carcass in a pressure cooker and add the water, 1 onion stuck with the cloves, 1 roughly-chopped stick of celery and the peppercorns. If you are using tinned celery, drain the liquid and reserve. Cover and cook on high pressure for 20 minutes. Release the pressure according to the manufacturer's instructions and strain the stock through a sieve into a large bowl. Stir in the drained juice from the tinned celery, if using. When the carcass is cool enough, carefully remove and discard the bones and add the flesh to the stock. Finely chop the remaining vegetables.

Return the stock to the pressure cooker and add the vegetables, the juice of half a lemon and the lemon rind. Check the seasoning. Bring to high pressure and cook for a further 5 minutes, then release the pressure. Just before serving, add the dumplings to the simmering stock and cook for about 10 minutes. Take care not to overcook the dumplings or they will become hard and rubbery.

SPECIAL OLIVES

Olives marinated in this way will keep for several months even without refrigeration. For the finest flavour, good-quality olive oil should be used but I have made it using vegetable oil with an almost equal degree of success. The longer you allow the olives to steep the better they will taste. The oil will add a wonderful flavour if used in salad dressings or chicken dishes as well as brushed over bass or mullet when grilling them.

SERVES 6

**225 g (8 oz) black olives (if they are   2 small slices of lemon peel
    in brine, drained)   olive oil
1–2 cloves garlic, peeled and
    quartered   1 large empty coffee jar or
2 rounded teaspoons dried   container with lid
    oregano *or* thyme**

Put the olives into the jar and add the garlic, oregano or thyme and lemon peel, leaving about an 1.25 cm (½ in) gap at the top of the jar. Pour over enough oil to cover the olives and shake well. Marinate for at least 12 hours – if you can keep them out of reach for that long!

KIPPER FILLETS

This recipe is delicious made with the genuine article but is also quite acceptable using a tin of kipper fillets. It makes a very good starter if served on toast or rye bread.

SERVES 4

**4 kipper fillets *or* 1 tin boned   1 tablespoon freshly chopped
    kipper fillets   parsley
juice of ½ a lemon   black pepper**

Remove the skin from each fillet; with the point of a sharp knife ease the skin away from the flesh at the tail end. Then slip your fingers underneath to help get a firm grip and gently pull from tail to head, removing the skin completely. Cut the fillets into long strips as thinly as possible. Put the fillets in a small bowl and pour over the lemon juice. Sprinkle with the parsley and black pepper. Leave to marinate for at least two hours. Drain and serve on toast or rye bread.

SARDINES FLAMBÉ

Ewen Southby-Tailyour   *BLACK VELVET II*

Ewen is an extremely experienced yachtsman and a major in the Royal Marines. During the Falklands campaign he was the advisor to the commander of the 3rd Commando Brigade who was in charge of the Task Force Landing Squadron.

Ewen told me the following story about this recipe: 'In 1979 I was the navigator of a motor yacht taking part in the search for John Paul Jones's flagship the *Bonnehomme Richard* in the North Sea. We had conducted months of research into the weather, tidal and sea conditions prevailing on the day she was set adrift following a successful action against the British ship the *Serapis* in the Battle of Flamborough Head in 1779. She had drifted for 36 hours before sinking. Our search lasted some weeks using magnatometers and sidescan sonors and I had also previously carried out a drift study for 36 hours from the last-known position of the *Bonnehomme Richard*.'

'Months later I was sent the official report of the expedition in which I suppose I had expected some mention to be made of the time I had devoted to navigational practice and research. However, the only reference to me was at the end of the report and said: ". . . those long hours were monotonous and uncomfortable and were relieved by Ewen's talent for marinating sardines in gin and pouring whisky over our porridge." Since we failed to find the wreck I think it was quite right that it was the only praise the navigators received.'

Ewen says that his record of eating nothing but sardines washed down with the occasional glass of whisky is eleven days (he was single-handed at the time). A word of warning before trying this recipe: it is best to choose a quiet day or make sure that you are fully clothed even if the weather is hot.

SERVES 1

1 slice bread
110 g (4 oz) tin sardines in oil
1 tablespoon gin

Lightly toast the bread on both sides. Butter the toast and empty the contents of the tin on top. Hold the tablespoon of gin over a flame until it ignites. Pour over the sardines and wait until the flame dies out. Serve immediately.

STUFFED AVOCADOS

Eve Bonham   *GOING GOING . . .*

Eve and her mother, Diana, took part in the 1983 AZAB (Azores and Back Race) in their Contessa 32 *Going Going . . .* Before leaving they bought plenty of avocados in various stages of ripeness (some were bullet hard) and tucked them away wrapped in sweaters and woolly hats. The avocados formed Eve's staple diet in calm weather and apparently the gin and fresh lemons ran out long before the avocados!

SERVES 2

2 ripe but firm avocado pears
a little lemon juice
110 g (4 oz) tin of crab meat,
** flaked *or* prawns, drained**
4 tablespoons prawn cocktail
** sauce**

dash of chilli sauce
½ small green pepper, deseeded and
** finely chopped**
black pepper

Cut the avocados in half lengthways. Twist to loosen the stone and separate. Remove the stone. Brush with a little lemon juice to prevent the avocados from discolouring.

Mix together the crab meat or prawns with the prawn cocktail sauce and chilli sauce in a bowl. Fill each half of the avocado with this mixture, piling it up into the centre. Sprinkle with the chopped pepper and a little black pepper. Serve immediately with brown bread and butter.

MUTINY EGGS

Ewen Southby-Tailyour   *BLACK VELVET II*

Ewen says: 'One of my meals was the cause of a mutiny although the reason for my crew's behaviour was not revealed for some years. We were taking part in the 1970 Round Britain Race and entering Lerwick Harbour after a difficult passage from Barra around Muckle Flugga. The yacht was the 50-foot yawl *Speedwell of Cremyl*. As we came to the anchorage off the quay we didn't have much time to get ashore before the pubs shut. There was no time for argument or discussion. At the appropriate moment I shouted for the anchor to be let go but nothing happened.'

'My one crew, Roger, refused to co-operate and continued preparing the dinghy for launching. Eventually when he was ready he rowed himself to shore leaving me to sort things out. We met later in a hotel and all was well. Four years later at a dinner party he finally told me the cause of his mutiny. I had put too much garlic on his eggs at breakfast; it proved to be the final straw and Roger felt very strongly about it!'

Perhaps this version might have been better!

SERVES 2

a little oil
2 slices of stale bread
30 g (1 oz) butter
2–4 eggs
1 large onion, finely chopped

1–2 cloves garlic, crushed
1 tablespoon freshly chopped
  parsley
black pepper

Heat the oil in a frying pan and fry the bread on both sides. Remove with a slotted spoon and keep warm. Add the onion and garlic and fry gently for a few minutes, or until the onion is soft and beginning to brown. Remove the onion and garlic and divide equally between the two slices of fried bread.

Melt the butter in the pan, crack the eggs into the pan and fry gently in the normal way. Slide the eggs onto the fried bread and onion mixture and sprinkle with freshly chopped parsley and black pepper.

CACKLEBERRY PIE

Robert Nickerson   *RJN MARINE*

Robert is a farmer so he always takes a lot of fresh eggs (cackleberries) with him when he goes sailing. This kind of dish is an excellent way of using up leftovers, a sort of hash with eggs which is easily made whether calm or rough and the variations are almost unlimited.

SERVES 2

55 g (2 oz) butter or margarine
1 medium onion, sliced
2 cooked potatoes, sliced
6 eggs
salt and pepper
170 g (6 oz) cold meat, diced (for
    example, bully beef, cold ham
    or tongue)

170 g (6 oz) leftover vegetables,
    diced or a small tin of mixed
    vegetables, drained
55 g (2 oz) tin of anchovies,
    drained (optional)
85 g (3 oz) grated cheese

Melt the butter in a frying pan, add the onion and potatoes and cook gently for
about 5 minutes, or until the onion is soft. Crack the eggs into a bowl, season
well and whisk until frothy. Increase the heat a little and add the eggs to the
pan. Draw the mixture back from the edge of the pan into the middle until the
mixture is just beginning to set. Add the vegetables and meat. If you are using
anchovies, arrange them in a lattice pattern on the top. Cook over a low heat
for about 5 minutes, or until nearly set.

Sprinkle with the grated cheese and place under a preheated hot grill until
the pie is golden brown and just beginning to rise. If you are eating it with
your fingers, cut it into wedges or, if you are eating off a plate, cut it in half.

SPANISH OMELETTE

Ann Frazer   *GOLLYWOBBLER*

A quick and sustaining meal can be made out of the leftovers from the galley
and cooked in a frying pan with the addition of two or three eggs – it is then
called a Spanish omelette. The authentic Spanish omelette should include
potato and garlic, is usually between 1.25 and 2 cm (½ and ¾ in) thick and is
served not folded but flat.

SERVES 4

1 tablespoon oil
1 tablespoon butter
4 streaky rashers of bacon, cut
    into 2.5 cm (1 in) lengths
3 large boiled potatoes, diced
2 large onions, sliced

1 small green pepper, deseeded
    and sliced
2 cloves garlic, peeled and
    chopped
5 large eggs
salt and pepper

Heat the oil and butter together in a frying pan and add the bacon. Cook on a low heat until the fat runs and the bacon is just beginning to brown. Stir in the potatoes, onions, pepper and garlic. Cover the pan with a tightly-fitting lid and cook gently, shaking the pan from time to time, until the vegetables are soft but not browned.

Crack the eggs into a bowl, season well and whisk until frothy. Increase the heat a little and add the eggs to the pan. Fry gently for about 3–4 minutes and, as the egg sets at the edge of the pan, draw the mixture back gently with the fork to allow some of the egg on the surface to run underneath. (At this stage you are supposed to try and turn the omelette over to brown the uncooked side – under way this could cause the loss of one omelette!) If you have a grill, finish the omelette by putting the frying pan under the grill for a few seconds to set the top and lightly brown it. The omelette should be set but still moist.

EMPANADAS

Maralyn Bailey   *AURALYN II*

Empanadas are a type of fried pasty and can be either sweet or savoury. They are a traditional Chilean dish but are found in most Spanish-speaking countries and are one of Maralyn's favourite shipboard dishes. She says that you should avoid using tinned pie fillings that contain a liquid gravy or syrup since it will be difficult to prevent it bursting out from the pastry during the cooking.

SERVES 4

285 g (10 oz) plain flour and
   2 teaspoons baking powder *or*
   285 g (10 oz) self-raising flour
55 g (2 oz) butter or margarine
2–4 tablespoons cold water
oil for frying

For the filling:
Savoury – 400 g (14 oz) corned
   beef and mashed potato *or*
   cheese and onion *or* ham *or* fish
Sweet – 400 g (14 oz) tin of black
   cherries *or* blackberry and
   apple *or* blackcurrants

Sift the flour and, if you are using it, the baking powder into a large bowl. Cut the butter or margarine into small dice and add them to the flour. Rub in the fat, using your fingertips, until the mixture looks like fine breadcrumbs.

Sprinkle a tablespoon of the water at a time over the flour mixture. Mix lightly together, adding a little more water if necessary to make a firm dough.

Divide the dough into 8 portions. Roll each portion out on a lightly-floured surface to a circle 18 cm (7 in) in diameter. Divide the filling equally and place in the centre of each circle and draw the two opposite sides together over the filling. Be careful over the amount of filling you use for each one as it might leak out during the cooking time. Press the edges firmly together over the top of the filling.

Heat enough oil in a frying pan so that it is 1.25 cm (½ in) deep until it sizzles. If the sea is fairly rough and the boat rolling about a lot, reduce the amount of oil for safety. Put 3 or 4 empanadas into the pan and fry for 3–4 minutes, basting constantly with a spoon. If the motion of the boat dictates shallow oil, keep turning to allow them to brown on all sides. Top up the pan with oil after each pan of empanadas is cooked.

TUNA SPAGHETTI

Richard and Maura Fanshawe   *ZERLINA*

SERVES 4–6

170 g (6 oz) tin of tuna in oil, drained and the oil reserved
1 tablespoon olive oil
55 g (2 oz) butter
1–2 cloves garlic, finely chopped
250 ml (8 fl oz) chicken stock

3 tablespoons dry white wine or vermouth
salt and pepper
450 g (1 lb) spaghetti
freshly chopped parsley to garnish

Heat the oil and half of the butter together in a large saucepan and add the garlic. Fry gently for 1–2 minutes. Stir in the oil from the tuna, stock and wine or vermouth. Cook on a high heat, bringing to the boil, until the liquid has reduced by about a half (about 150 ml or ¼ pint). Break the tuna into flakes and add to the liquid. Check the seasoning and simmer for 5 minutes.

Cook the spaghetti, uncovered, in plenty of boiling salted water and drain it as soon as it is tender – about 10 minutes. Melt the remainder of the butter in the saucepan and return the spaghetti to the pan. Toss the spaghetti in the butter, pour over the sauce and sprinkle with freshly chopped parsley. Serve immediately with a green salad.

SPAGHETTI ALLA CARBONARA

Richard and Maura Fanshawe   *ZERLINA*

SERVES 5–6

170 g (6 oz) streaky bacon
15 g (½ oz) butter
450 g (1 lb) spaghetti

3 large eggs
salt and pepper
Parmesan cheese to taste

Cut the bacon into thin strips or dice, melt the butter in a pan and add the bacon. Cook gently until the fat runs and the bacon is crisp. Remove the bacon with a slotted spoon, drain it on kitchen paper and keep warm.

Cook the spaghetti, uncovered, in plenty of boiling salted water and drain it as soon as it is tender – about 10 minutes. Remove from the heat. Crack the eggs into a bowl, beat well and then pour over the spaghetti, stirring constantly, until the egg has set. Return the bacon to the pan, season and mix well. Serve immediately, handing around the Parmesan separately.

JURA HASH

Martin Muncaster   *COTTONTAIL*

SERVES 4

30 g (1 oz) butter
2–3 small onions, finely chopped
1–2 cloves garlic, crushed
400 g (14 oz) tin of tomatoes
225 g (8 oz) spaghetti

312 g (11 oz) tin of corned beef, diced
1 tablespoon cornflour
salt and pepper
1 tablespoon olive oil
freshly chopped parsley

Melt the butter in a saucepan and add the onions and garlic. Fry gently until they are soft, but not browned. Add the tomatoes and their juice and the corned beef, breaking the tomatoes up with a wooden spoon. Bring to the boil, reduce the heat to low and simmer gently for about 10 minutes. If the sauce looks rather thin, thicken with the cornflour slackened with a tablespoon of water or sauce. Season.

Cook the spaghetti, uncovered, in plenty of boiling salted water and drain it as soon as it is tender – about 10 minutes. Mix in the oil and parsley. Tip the pasta into a large, heated serving bowl and pour over the hash. Serve immediately with a crisp green salad and a full-bodied red wine.

BAKED MACKEREL IN FOIL

Liz Hammick   *WRESTLER OF LEIGH*

After catching your mackerel make sure they are laid out straight to stiffen and are not left curled in a bucket.

SERVES 4

4 freshly-caught mackerel	pinch of fresh *or* dried mixed
1 large onion, finely chopped *or*	herbs
1 tablespoon dehydrated onion	1 tablespoon lemon juice, fresh or
flakes	bottled
1 large green pepper, deseeded	salt and pepper
and finely chopped *or* 1 dried	
red pepper	

Clean and gut the fish as described on page 24, removing the backbone. Cut off the head, tail and fins and clean with salt water.

Mix together the onion, pepper, herbs and lemon juice in a bowl. Season well. Fill each mackerel with this mixture and then press back into shape. Wrap each in an individual piece of buttered aluminium foil and then place on a baking tray and bake in a preheated hot oven (220°C/425°F, gas mark 7) for about 20–25 minutes depending on the size of the fish. Gently prod the fish with a fork and if it flakes easily it is cooked. It should not be overdone. Serve immediately with a hunk of French bread, boiled potatoes and a salad.

Any fish that is leftover can be flaked and mixed with a tablespoon of mayonnaise and seasonings and eaten cold as a pâté. One advantage of this recipe is that it leaves the minimum of washing up, unlike frying or grilling, and also reduces cooking smells.

SOUSED MACKEREL

Richard Clifford   *WARRIOR SHAMAAL*

This is a good way of preserving fresh fish if you have caught too many to eat at once or simply want to souse them for future use as, this way, they will keep for at least six weeks.

SERVES 8

8 small to medium mackerel, pollack *or* herring	2 tablespoons mixed pickling spice
1 large onion, chopped	black pepper
600 ml (1 pint) malt vinegar	
600 ml (1 pint) sea water *or* fresh water and 1 tablespoon salt	toothpicks

Clean, bone and fillet each fish as described on page 24. Roll up each fillet from tail to head, skin outwards, with some onion in the middle. Secure each fillet with half a toothpick and place them fairly close together in a large saucepan. Sprinkle with the pickling spice and the pepper (freshly ground if available).

Mix together equal amounts of salt water and vinegar in a measuring jug and then pour over enough of the liquid to cover the fish. Bring to the boil and simmer gently for about 5 minutes. Remove from the heat and allow to cool in the liquid. When cold store in an airtight jar or plastic container and make sure that the fish is covered with the liquid.

CHICKEN WITH OLIVES AND WINE

SERVES 4–6

1.35–1.6 kg (3–3½ lb) chicken	1 large potato, diced
3–4 tablespoons olive oil	pinch of dried oregano *or* thyme
1–2 cloves garlic, peeled and quartered	150 ml (¼ pint) dry white wine
	6–8 black olives
2 ripe tomatoes, peeled and quartered	black pepper
2–3 courgettes, cut into 6 mm (¼ in) slices	

Joint the chicken into 8–10 pieces, cutting the thigh and drumstick in half at the joint. Arrange the chicken pieces in an ovenproof dish and pour over the oil. (For a really robust flavour you can use the oil from the recipe for Special Olives, see page 77.) Tuck the pieces of garlic between the chicken pieces and then add the courgettes and potato.

If you wish to peel the tomatoes, plunge them into boiling water for 1 minute, then drain and peel away the skins. Quarter the tomatoes and add to the casserole. Sprinkle with the oregano or thyme and olives and pour over the wine. Cook in a preheated hot oven (200°C/400°F, gas mark 6) for 45 minutes, turning and basting the chicken with the juices halfway and three-quarters through the cooking time. The chicken should be tender and the skin crisp and golden brown. The potatoes should be just beginning to brown. Serve the chicken on a bed of noodles with the vegetables and sauce piled on top.

MACKEREL IN WHITE WINE

Ann Frazer *GOLLYWOBBLER*

This is another excellent way of cooking mackerel, especially when the fishermen have been over energetic, as poached or baked like this the fish will keep until the next day even if you don't have a fridge. It is good hot or cold.

SERVES 4

4 freshly-caught mackerel
For the Court Bouillon:
2 small onions, sliced
2 medium carrots, thinly sliced
200 ml (⅓ pint) white wine
100 ml (3½ fl oz) white wine
   vinegar
1 bay leaf
5 black peppercorns

½ teaspoon fennel seeds
1 dessertspoon freshly chopped
   chives *or* 1 teaspoon dried
   chives
1 dessertspoon freshly chopped
   parsley *or* 1 teaspoon dried
   parsley
1 teaspoon salt
1 tablespoon olive oil

Clean and gut the fish as described on page 24. Cut off the head and tail or not as desired and clean with salt water. Put in an ovenproof dish and set aside while you prepare the *court bouillon.*

Put all the remaining ingredients into a saucepan and slowly bring to the boil. Reduce the heat, cover and simmer for about 20 minutes. Pour the *court bouillon* over the fish and cover with aluminium foil.* Bake in a preheated moderately hot oven (200°C/400°F, gas mark 6) for 20 minutes. Remove from the oven and allow to cool. If the mackerel are not going to be eaten until the next day, keep them in their liquid and covered with the aluminium foil.

Before serving, remove them from the *court bouillon* with a slotted spoon which can be discarded. Serve with a green salad and new potatoes which have been tossed, while still warm, in a dressing of olive oil, chives and a little vinegar.

If you don't have an oven, the fish can be poached on top of the stove in a saucepan.

CHICKEN STEW

Nigel Rowe   SEA TROLL

SERVES 2

2 chicken breasts *or* similar
 quantity of turkey, skinned and
 cut into large cubes
1 tablespoon oil
30 g (1 oz) butter
2 large onions, thickly sliced
1 green pepper, deseeded and
 sliced
4 tomatoes, peeled and quartered
 or 200 g (7 oz) tin of tomatoes,
 drained

6 cloves garlic, roughly chopped
1 tablespoon soy sauce
120 ml (4 fl oz) dry sherry
generous pinch of mixed dried
 herbs
salt and pepper
450 g (1 lb) tin of potatoes, drained

Heat the oil and butter together in a large saucepan, add the onions and cook them on a low heat until they are soft, but not browned. Remove the onions with a slotted spoon and reserve. Add the cubes of chicken or turkey and quickly brown on all sides. Return the onions to the pan and add the pepper, tomatoes, garlic, soy sauce, sherry and mixed herbs. Bring to the boil, then reduce the heat to a simmer, cover the pan tightly and cook for about 20 minutes.

Check the seasoning and add the potatoes, stirring well. Simmer for a further 10 minutes. Serve with crusty bread and a dry white wine. Nigel recommends a Chablis.

CARIBBEAN-STYLE CHICKEN

Ann Frazer   *GOLLYWOBBLER*

Ann spent a year cruising in the Caribbean and this is her version of that region's chicken dish.

SERVES 6

1.35–1.8 kg (3–4 lb) chicken
3 tablespoons oil
1 large onion, sliced
1–2 teaspoons mild curry powder
  or paste
2 cloves garlic, crushed
1–2 small hot red chillis, deseeded
  and chopped
400 g (14 oz) tin of water chestnuts,
  drained

425 g (15 oz) tin of pineapple
  chunks in natural juice
425 g (15 oz) tin of tomatoes
400 g (14 oz) tin of green beans,
  drained
1 dessertspoon chopped fresh
  chives
salt and pepper

With a sharp knife joint the chicken into 8 pieces, slicing through the natural crease to divide the thigh from the drumstick. Heat the oil in a heavy saucepan, add the chicken pieces and fry until evenly browned on all sides. Remove the chicken from the pan and set aside. Reduce the heat, add the onion and fry gently until it is soft, but not browned. Stir in the curry powder or paste, garlic and chillis and fry gently for about 3–4 minutes.

Return the chicken to the pan and add the water chestnuts, pineapple, tomatoes and their juice. Break up the tomatoes with a fork and season well. Bring up to the boil, reduce the heat, cover and simmer for about 35 minutes, or until the chicken is tender. Check the seasoning, stir in the green beans and chives and cook for a further 5 minutes. Serve on a bed of plain, boiled rice with a green salad.

SMOTHERED CHICKEN

Penny Bourne   *EILA ROSE*

Mozzarella cheese is now easily obtainable in sealed packets from most of the large supermarkets and it keeps very well if unopened. However, if unavailable, Gruyère or Emmenthal will do just as well for this recipe.

SERVES 2

2 chicken breasts
110 g (4 oz) butter
2 tablespoons tomato purée

2 teaspoons dried mixed herbs
2 thick slices of Mozzarella cheese

Remove and discard the skin from the chicken and arrange the chicken pieces in an ovenproof dish. Dot with half of the butter and bake in a preheated moderate oven (180°C/350°F, gas mark 4) for 20 minutes. Remove from the oven, spread the tomato purée over the chicken pieces, sprinkle with half of the herbs, then place a slice of cheese on each piece and dot with the remainder of the butter and herbs. Return to the oven for a further 25 minutes. Serve immediately with new potatoes and a crisp green salad.

CHILLI

John Martin   *MAINSTAY VOORTREKKA*

SERVES 1–2

2 tablespoons oil
1 large onion, roughly chopped
1 teaspoon curry powder
1–2 teaspoons chilli powder or
**   more to taste**
1–2 cloves garlic, finely chopped
310 g (11 oz) tin of bully beef, cut
**   into cubes**

400 g (14 oz) tin of tomato soup
400 g (14 oz) tin of baked beans
1 large green pepper, deseeded
**   and sliced**
salt and pepper

Heat the oil in a large saucepan, add the onion and cook until the onion is soft, but not browned. Stir in the curry powder, chilli and garlic and sauté gently for a few minutes to draw out the flavour of the curry and chilli powder. Add the beef, tomato soup, beans and pepper, mix well and slowly bring to the boil. Reduce the heat and simmer for about 20 minutes.

Check the seasoning, take the chilli off the heat and leave it to absorb the full flavour of the chilli powder for at least 6 hours before eating. Reheat it to just below boiling point and serve with a salad.

BOEUF À LA BOURNE

Edward Bourne   *EILA ROSE*

Edward raced with Bill Perks in the 1982 Round Britain and Ireland Race. During the 48-hour compulsory stop-over in Lerwick, Edward bought two excellent steaks for dinner on the evening that they had to leave behind the generous hospitality of the Shetlanders to face the rigours of the North Sea. As they left the lights of Lerwick behind them, Bill was on watch while Edward was down below creating this dish using a foil packet of minced beef and onions as the basis of a wonderful 'Bordelaise' sauce.

SERVES 2

2 T-bone or rump steaks
30 g (1 oz) butter
2 medium onions, roughly chopped
1 clove garlic, finely chopped
110 g (4 oz) fresh mushrooms,
    sliced *or* 140 g (5 oz) tin of
    mushrooms, drained

1 foil packet of minced beef and
    onions
120 ml (4 fl oz) red wine
pinch of mixed dried herbs
salt and pepper

Melt the butter in a pan and fry the onions and garlic until they are soft, but not browned. Stir in the mushrooms and the contents of the foil packet. Bring to the boil and add the wine and herbs, then reduce the heat and simmer gently while you cook the steaks.

You can either grill or fry the steaks. First trim the steaks and pat them dry. To grill them: place under a preheated hot grill, brown them for 1 minute each side, reduce the heat slightly and continue to cook for 3–4 minutes. To fry them: heat 30 g (1 oz) butter in a heavy frying pan, add the steaks as soon as the first side is sealed and reduce the heat. Turn them halfway through the cooking time. The time they will take to cook will depend on the thickness of the meat and how well done you like them. Check the seasoning of the sauce and as soon as the steaks are done, pour it over the meat. Serve immediately with plain, boiled potatoes and eat in reverent silence.

THE HAGGIS

Valentine Thornhill *SAI SEE*

I am no haggis expert! However, Valentine assures me that on no account should a haggis be boiled. She says that if you cook it, like this, in an oven it will come out with a crisp rather than soggy edge.

SERVES 2
1 haggis

Prick the haggis all over with a fork. Place it on a rack in a roasting tin to catch the excess fat. Cook in a preheated moderate oven (180°C/350°F, gas mark 4) for 45 minutes. Increase the temperature to moderately hot (200°C/400°F, gas mark 6) and cook for a further 20 minutes.

Serve with grilled tomatoes and wash down with a large glass of your favourite malt whisky.

SLUMGULLION OR SHIP'S STEW

' "There ain't nothin to jaw about with this fair wind, cap'n," he argued. "We had a good trip so far. Only one man, that Swede had to be put in irons for trying to kill the cook." Swede had caught the cook in the act of putting a dead cat into the slumgullion, as ship's stew is termed. Cook was holding out the salt beef for himself and pawning off the dead pussy. Taking fo'c's'le justice in his own hands Swede caught cook by the back of the neck and began to shake the liver out of him. The cook managed to get his meat cleaver and attempted to assassinate Swede. There would have been a dual murder in the galley if Bulgar and Oleson hadn't intervened in time. Father put Swede in irons for attempted murder, but we needed cook, so all that happened to him for bad conduct was forfeiture of one month's pay.' (*Cradle of the Deep*, Joan Lowell, Simon and Schuster 1920)

SERVES 8

1.8 kg (4 lb) salted beef, silverside or topside	2 small onions, studded with 2 whole cloves each
150 ml (¼ pint) beef stock *or* beer	2 sticks of celery, halved
2 bay leaves	8 medium onions, peeled and quartered
2 cloves garlic, peeled	8 medium carrots, cut in half lengthways and halved again
2 tablespoons freshly chopped parsley or 2 teaspoons dried parsley	4 medium potatoes, peeled and halved
1 teaspoon dried thyme	
8 black peppercorns	
8 juniper berries, crushed	8 dumplings (see below)

Put the beef, herbs, cloved onions and celery sticks in a pressure cooker and pour over the stock or beer and enough fresh, cold water to cover. Bring to the boil, uncovered, and remove any scum from the surface. Cover and cook according to the manufacturer's instructions for 1 hour 10 minutes, then release the steam slowly.

Remove the beef and set aside. Strain the liquid and return to the pressure cooker along with the remainder of the vegetables. Cook on high pressure for a further 6 minutes, release the pressure and cook the dumplings as described below. Transfer the beef to a heated serving dish and surround it with the vegetables and dumplings. Hand round the stock separately.

ENGLISH DUMPLINGS

Maralyn Bailey   *AURALYN II*

Dumplings can turn an ordinary tin of stew into a satisfying meal which is an ideal one-pot dish for rough weather. They make a change from potatoes and are cooked in the stew itself. It is important to serve the dumplings straight-away as they become rubbery if left.

SERVES 4

110 g (4 oz) plain flour	55 g (2 oz) shredded suet
1 teaspoon baking powder	cold water to mix
½ teaspoon salt	

Sift the flour, baking powder and salt into a bowl and add the suet, mixing well with a fork. Stirring the mixture with a round-bladed knife, add enough water to make a firm dough. (If you are using sea water omit the ½ teaspoon of salt.) Shape the dough into 6–8 small dumplings, flouring your hands to prevent the mixture from sticking, and roll into balls. Drop the dumplings into a soup or stew which must be simmering. Cook them in simmering stock for about 10–15 minutes depending on their size.

STEW

Rachael Hayward *LOIWING*

Rachael Hayward recently crossed the Mediterranean from Libya to Malta via the Greek Islands during the two hottest months in the Mediterranean, July and August. This stew formed the crew of five's staple diet and it was added to and kept going for a couple of days or more without refrigeration.

For supper each day fresh ingredients were added to the original stew. After supper, the stew was brought to high pressure for five minutes and then left to cool. Provided that the seal is *not* broken or the weight removed the contents will keep for two to three days.

SERVES 4–6

110 g (4 oz) freeze-dried peas *or*
   runner beans
2 tablespoons oil
4 large onions, sliced
2 cloves garlic, chopped
900 g (2 lb) stewing steak

seasoned flour
4 large carrots, sliced
1 tablespoon tomato purée
bouquet garni
1 litre (1¾ pints) beef stock
salt and pepper

Put the dried vegetables into a bowl and cover with 5 cm (2 in) of boiling water; cover with Cling Film and leave to soak for at least 30 minutes.

Heat the oil in a pressure cooker, add the onions and garlic and fry until lightly browned. Remove the onions with a slotted spoon and set aside. Dip the meat in the seasoned flour, add to the pressure cooker and fry until lightly browned on all sides. Return the onions to the pan and stir in the carrots, tomato purée, bouquet garni, strained vegetables and the stock, making sure that the meat is covered with the stock. Do not add any salt at this stage or it will make the dried vegetables very tough. Cover and cook on high pressure for 20 minutes. Release the pressure according to the manufacturer's instructions. Check the seasoning and serve immediately.

BAKED HAM

Tim and Mary Heywood   *LA MICHELLE*

SERVES 2

450 g (1 lb) tin of ham
8 whole cloves
1 tablespoon dark brown sugar

Scrape the jelly off the ham and stick the ham with the cloves. Dust with the sugar, wrap in aluminium foil and bake in a preheated moderately hot oven (200°C/400°F, gas mark 6) for 30 minutes. Serve with tinned potatoes and ready-made parsley sauce.

CHOPPED HAM

John Gore-Grimes   *SHARDANA*

Tinned hams tend to be rather on the salty side so scrape off the jelly and take care with the seasoning.

SERVES 4

450 g (1 lb) tin of ham, chopped
1 tablespoon oil
1 medium onion, chopped
½ green pepper, deseeded and chopped
½ sweet red pepper, deseeded and chopped
200 g (7 oz) tin of mushrooms, drained

400 g (14 oz) tin of peas *or* mixed vegetables, drained
400 g (14 oz) tin of tomato *or* mushroom soup
pinch of mixed dried herbs
black pepper
2 tablespoons single cream or top of the milk (optional)

Heat the oil in a large saucepan and add the onion. Cook on a low heat until the onion is soft, but not browned. Add the peppers and fry for a few minutes more and then stir in all the vegetables, the ham, tinned soup and mixed herbs. Bring to the boil, season lightly with pepper, cover the pan and simmer for about 20 minutes. Stir the mixture from time to time to check that it is not becoming too thick and add a little water if it is. It should be a creamy consistency.

Just before serving check the seasoning and stir in the cream or top of the milk, if you are using it. Serve immediately with boiled brown rice.

SWEET AND SOUR PORK

Bumble Ogilvy-Wedderburn   *ADC ACCUTRAC*

If you are lucky enough to have a deep freeze on board, then this is a simple and delicious main course using a shoulder of pork which is an economical joint to use. If you do not have a freezer on board then this dish is almost as good made with a tin of ham or, perhaps, vacuum-packed gammon steaks.

SERVES 4–5

900 g (2 lb) shoulder of pork *or*
  900 g (2 lb) tin of ham
a little flour
2 tablespoons oil
3 large onions, sliced
2 tablespoons cornflour
400 g (14 oz) tin of tomatoes
225 g (8 oz) tin of pineapple
  chunks, in natural juice

1–2 tablespoons Worcestershire
  sauce
1–2 teaspoons sugar
lemon juice, fresh or bottled
salt and pepper
1 green pepper, deseeded and
  chopped

The method of preparation is slightly different depending on whether you are using fresh pork or tinned ham. If you are using fresh pork, trim off the excess fat. Cut the pork into even-sized cubes and dust with a little flour. Heat the oil in a flameproof casserole, add the pork and brown it evenly on all sides. Take out the meat and set aside. Add the onions and fry until browned, but without allowing them to burn. Return the pork to the pan, reduce the heat and sprinkle with the cornflour, stirring well. Add the tomatoes and their juice, pineapple juice from the tin, Worcestershire sauce, sugar and lemon juice and stir well.

Bring up to the boil, reduce the heat, cover with a tightly-fitting lid and simmer for about 30 minutes, or until the pork is tender. Check the seasoning, adding more sugar or salt as necessary to make it taste sharp and sweet. When the meat is tender, add the pepper and pineapple chunks and simmer for a further 5 minutes. The peppers should be crunchy. Serve with plain, boiled rice.

If you are using tinned ham, heat the oil in a pan and add the onions. Fry gently until browned, but without allowing them to burn. Add the cornflour, tomatoes and their juice, pineapple juice and seasonings and simmer for about 10–15 minutes, or until the onions are soft. Go carefully on the salt as tinned ham tends to be very salty. Cut the tinned ham into cubes and add to the pan with the pepper and pineapple chunks and simmer for a further 5 minutes, or until the ham is heated through.

GRILLED PORK CHOPS WITH CIDER

SERVES 2

2 pork loin chops	200 ml (⅓ pint) dry cider
1 tablespoon seasoned flour	1 dessertspoon brown sugar
½ teaspoon ground coriander	dash of calvados (optional)
1 medium onion, finely chopped	
2 medium apples, peeled and finely sliced	

Trim the chops of any excess fat and score with a knife on either side. Dip the chops in the seasoned flour to which you have added the ground coriander. Press half of the onion on top of the chops and put them in the grill pan without the grid. Place under a preheated hot grill for about 7 minutes, turn and cover with the remainder of the onion and grill for a further 7 minutes, without allowing the onion to burn.

Remove the grill pan from the grill and put it on top of the stove over a moderate heat. Top the chops with the apple and cider and sprinkle them with the sugar. Continue to cook for about 4–6 minutes, or until the apples are soft but not browned. Baste the chops and if the mixture looks a little too dry, add some more cider. Just before serving, add a dash of calvados if you are using it. As this is a rich dish it is best served with plain, boiled rice and a salad.

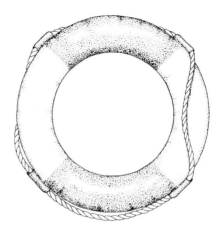

HASH

Hammond Innes   *MARY DEARE*

When asked to contribute a recipe, Hammond wrote back: 'A hash for all seasons, that's what this is. You mash some potatoes, shred in as many tins of corned beef as required, in the meantime frying up a mix of onions and bacon, and anything else you fancy, or you find lying around waiting to go bad or fall into the bilges; the usual seasoning (nothing ventured . . . be brave and experiment with some of the less usual if you like – a touch of chilli, even a little curry powder perhaps). Then mix the whole lot together.'

'The joy of hash is that it can be done in advance, before you row off for drinks on that other yacht, or in anticipation of a night sail, or just before you head out of the anchorage into Force 5, wind against tide and a nasty, steep little sea. Then, when the time comes for energy renewal, the whole mix is tipped into a fat-sizzling frying pan. Press it down firmly, turn it when crusty and you finish up with what looks like a huge rissole. Leave it in the pan to keep hot, cutting it like a cake – the second watch gets it as hot as the first, and within reason the crustier it gets the better it is.'

'Corned Beef Hash or American Hash – some people call it Red Flannel Hash, but that's because they put beetroot in it (I never had beetroot on board *Mary Deare*) – is for me one of the great sailing stand-bys. Force 7 or over you need meals in mugs, but hash will see you through a lot of bad weather with a minimum of fuss. As a kid I remember feasting on sardines and sweet condensed milk! An odd mix, the memory of which makes me wonder how a dash of anchovies would do in the hash. We had a Maltese friend, who, when we were sailing *Mary Deare* in the Mediterranean, liked to anchovise pasta sauces. Hash, like pasta is a "wittel" to play around with, and a wee dram of the malt afterwards doesn't do any harm.'

'I can almost hear you say afterwards – why not hash flambé au us-quebaugh!'

CORNED BEEF HASH

Jeff Houlgrave   COLT CARS

SERVES 1

200 g (7 oz) tin of corned beef, diced
200 g (7 oz) tin of butter beans, drained
1–2 teaspoons made mustard
1 tablespoon dehydrated potato powder

150 ml (¼ pint) boiling water
Worcestershire sauce
salt and pepper

1 tablespoon oil

Mix together the corned beef, butter beans and mustard in a bowl. In a small bowl stir the boiling water into the potato powder and then add to the corned beef mixture. Season to taste with Worcestershire sauce and salt and pepper.

Heat the oil in a frying pan until it sizzles and then tip in the hash, flattening it down with the back of a wooden spoon. Gently fry until a golden brown crust forms on the underside and turn once. Cook for about 10 minutes on each side. Serve immediately.

VEGETABLE CURRY

Bumble Ogilvy-Wedderburn   ADC ACCUTRAC

Bumble's real name is Elizabeth but she is always known as Bumble. This is one of her 'Round the World' curries which was extremely popular with the crew. One of its advantages is that it can be made in any type of weather.

SERVES 6–8

15 g (½ oz) butter	2 medium potatoes, diced
2 large onions, sliced	1 green pepper, deseeded and
1 teaspoon ground cumin seeds	sliced
1 teaspoon ground ginger	425 g (15 oz) tin of tomatoes and
1 teaspoon ground coriander	their juice
seeds	2–3 cloves garlic, crushed
2 teaspoons curry powder *or*	2 tablespoons mango chutney
paste or more according to taste	900 ml (1½ pints) water
225 g (8 oz) lentils	salt and pepper

Melt the butter in a large saucepan and add the onions, spices and curry powder or paste. Fry gently, stirring well, until the onions are soft, but not browned. Stir in the remainder of the ingredients. Bring to the boil, reduce the heat, cover and simmer gently for about 30 minutes, or until the lentils and potatoes are quite tender. Check the seasoning and serve with plain, boiled rice and natural yoghurt.

STUFFED PEPPERS

John Gore-Grimes   *SHARDANA*

SERVES 4

4 red or green peppers	200 g (7 oz) tin of mushrooms,
1 dessertspoon oil	drained
1 small onion, finely chopped	170 g (6 oz) cooked rice
1 clove garlic, crushed	pinch of dried tarragon
200 g (7 oz) tin of tuna, drained	salt and pepper

Cut the tops off the peppers and remove the seeds with a teaspoon. Plunge them into a pan of boiling salted water and leave to blanch for 5 minutes. Remove and leave to drain upside down while you prepare the stuffing.

Heat the oil in a pan, add the onion and garlic and fry gently until it is soft, but not browned. Add the tuna, mushrooms, rice and seasonings and gently cook for about 5 minutes. Spoon the mixture into the peppers and stand them in a lightly-greased baking dish with about 2.5 cm (1 in) of water in the bottom. Bake in a preheated moderate oven (160°C/325°F, gas mark 3) for about 15–20 minutes.

PILLAU RICE

SERVES 4

225 g (8 oz) long grain rice
55 g (2 oz) butter
1 medium onion
1 teaspoon turmeric
4 whole cardamon pods

2–4 whole cloves
½ teaspoon ground cinnamon *or*
   5 cm (2 in) cinnamon stick
   broken in pieces
600 ml (1 pint) cold water

Melt the butter in a saucepan which has a well-fitting lid and add the onion. Gently fry the onion until it is just beginning to brown, but without allowing it to burn. Add the rice and spices and fry for a few more minutes, stirring constantly, until the rice is well coated and transparent. Add the water, bring the rice to the boil, reduce the heat to low and cover the pan. Simmer for about 12–15 minutes or until all the water is absorbed and the rice quite tender.

CURRIED FRENCH OR RUNNER BEANS

Richard Clifford   *WARRIOR SHAMAAL*

Fresh beans do not keep well on board, so this is an excellent way of preserving them to serve with cold meat or fish or simply on their own with a salad.

SERVES 6–8

1 medium onion, thinly sliced
boiling water
900 g (2 lb) beans, cubed or sliced
1½ tablespoons cornflour
½ tablespoon salt
1½ tablespoons curry powder, or
   more according to taste

750 ml (1¼ pints) white wine
   vinegar
340 g (12 oz) caster or granulated
   sugar

Put the onion into a bowl, pour over enough boiling water to cover, and set aside. Cook the beans in boiling salted water until they are quite tender but still crisp – about 10 minutes. Mix together the cornflour, salt and curry powder in a bowl with a little of the vinegar to make a smooth paste.

Put the remainder of the vinegar and sugar into a pan, bring up to the boil and simmer for 3 minutes stirring from time to time to dissolve the sugar. Remove from the heat and gradually stir in the curry and cornflour paste. Return to the heat and bring up to the boil. Reduce the heat and simmer for a further 3–5 minutes, stirring from time to time. Check the seasoning and allow to cool. When the sauce is cold, drain the onions and add with the beans to the sauce. Mix well and store in a jar or airtight plastic container.

RATATOUILLE

For authenticity, this popular French country stew should be cooked in the very best olive oil. It is equally delicious hot or cold.

120 ml (4 fl oz) olive oil
4 medium onions, sliced
2 large aubergines
450 g (1 lb) tomatoes
4 medium courgettes
2 green peppers, deseeded and
  sliced
2 red peppers, deseeded and
  sliced
1–2 sprigs of fresh chopped
  coriander *or* ½ teaspoon
  ground coriander *or* 1 teaspoon
  dried basil
salt and pepper

Heat the oil in a large pan and add the onions. Cover the pan and cook very slowly until the onions are soft, but not browned. Cut the aubergines into cubes, put in a colander and sprinkle with a generous amount of salt. Leave to drain. Cut the courgettes into 14 mm (½ in) slices and quarter the tomatoes. If you wish to peel the tomatoes, plunge them into a bowl of boiling water for 1 minute, then drain and peel away the skins.

Rinse the aubergines, pat dry on kitchen paper and add to the pan with the prepared peppers, courgettes, coriander or basil and top with tomatoes. Season well. Cover and cook very slowly for a further 40 minutes.

BREAD AND BUTTER PUDDING

'Spud' Spedding

Spud says his wife, Ros, who is as competent in the galley as he is useless, has cooked this dish in places as diverse as Antigua and the Outer Hebrides and it has always received high praise. The reason, he thinks, is that it appeals to the Englishman's prep-school palate. It is also an excellent way of finishing up stale sliced white bread and leftover longlife milk.

If you do not have any dried fruit available, spread the bread and butter with marmalade.

SERVES 4

**3–4 slices of stale, sliced bread
butter or margarine
55 g (2 oz) mixed dried fruit
55 g (2 oz) brown or white sugar
2 eggs**

**450 ml (¾ pint) milk
ground nutmeg *or* ground mixed
    spice to taste**

Butter the bread on one side only and cut the bread into thin slices. Arrange a layer at the bottom of a buttered ovenproof dish. Sprinkle the slices with the fruit and sugar and then repeat the layers finishing with a layer of bread and butter.

Crack the eggs into a bowl and beat lightly. Warm the milk in a pan and pour it onto the eggs, stirring briskly. Pour the milk mixture over the bread and butter and sprinkle the top with nutmeg or mixed spice. Allow the mixture to stand for 30 minutes. Bake in a preheated moderate oven (180°C/350°F, gas mark 4) for about 30–40 minutes or until the top is golden brown.

A VERY GOOD PUDDING

Bumble Ogilvy-Wedderburn   *ADC ACCUTRAC*

SERVES 4–6

**225 g (8 oz) plain flour
1 teaspoon baking powder
140 g (5 oz) butter
55 g (2 oz) caster sugar**

**1 egg, lightly beaten
300 ml (½ pint) milk
½ jar of jam, any flavour**

Sift together the flour and baking powder and set aside. Cream the butter and sugar until light and fluffy. Gradually beat the egg into the creamed mixture. Fold in half the flour, then the remaining flour and enough of the milk (about 1–2 tablespoons) to mix to a stiff paste. Roll out on a lightly-floured board to an oblong shape and then spread evenly with the jam.

Roll up and turn into a buttered oblong ovenproof dish. Pour over the rest of the milk and bake in a preheated moderately hot oven (190°C/375°F, gas mark 5) for 30 minutes, or until golden brown. Serve with custard or cream.

PEARS WITH CHOCOLATE SAUCE

Richard and Maura Fanshawe   *ZERLINA*

SERVES 6

6 ripe pears *or* 900 g (2 lb) tin of
   pear halves in natural juice,
   drained
2 Mars bars, sliced
2 tablespoons cold water

2 tablespoons lemon juice, fresh
   or bottled
1–2 tablespoons brandy *or*
   whisky

If using fresh pears, cut into halves and remove the cores. If using tinned pears, strain them carefully. Arrange the pear halves on individual plates, allowing two per person.

Put the slices of Mars bars into a small saucepan with 2 tablespoons of water and heat together very gently, stirring constantly. Gradually add the lemon juice until the sauce is thick and smooth. Just before serving stir in the alcohol and pour the sauce over the pears. Serve immediately with generous helpings of whipped cream, if available, to which you have added some brandy.

JUNKET

Laurel Holland

SERVES 4

600 ml (1 pint) milk
2 teaspoons rennet essence

1 tablespoon caster sugar
a little grated nutmeg

Heat the milk to about blood temperature (37°–38°C/98°–100°F) but no warmer. Put the rennet and sugar into a serving bowl and stir in the warm milk. Leave at room or 'galley' temperature to set. Sprinkle with nutmeg and serve with cream or stewed fruit.

ANY FOOL

Bumble Ogilvy-Wedderburn *ADC ACCUTRAC*

This dish is not quite as rich as the custard-based fool more often found in cookery books and neither does it require a pint of double cream. It is quick and easy to prepare in any weather conditions. Fruit tinned in its natural juices is less sweet and much nicer than syrup.

SERVES 6–8

2 425 g (15 oz) tins of soft fruit	2 eggs, separated
4 tablespoons fresh breadcrumbs	sugar to taste
55 g (2 oz) butter or margarine	1 egg white

Rub the contents of the tins through a sieve. (At home, process them briefly in a blender, and sieve the purée to remove any pips.)

Put the purée in a bowl and mix in the breadcrumbs. Melt the butter or margarine in a small saucepan over a low heat and then beat in the egg yolks and sugar. Add the mixture to the fruit and mix well. In a separate bowl mix the three egg whites until they hold a stiff peak and then fold into the fruit mixture. Serve with cream or custard.

HAZEL'S CAMEMBERT SAUCE

Bill and Hazel Perks *SHERPA BILL*

Hazel and Bill have sailed together throughout their married life, living in a variety of vessels ranging from a barge to their present yacht in which Bill successfully completed in the 1984 OSTAR. Hazel is an imaginative cook and the juxtaposition of tastes and textures from the smooth richness of the cheese to the sharpness of the fruit is quite remarkable.

SERVES 2–4

1 ripe Camembert cheese	lemon juice, fresh *or* bottled
2 ripe pears *or* 450 g (1 lb) tin of pear halves in natural juice, drained	4 tablespoons double *or* long life cream
	pinch of paprika

If using fresh pears, peel, cut into halves and remove the cores. Brush with a little lemon juice to stop them from turning brown. If using tinned pears, strain them carefully. Arrange the pear halves on individual plates, allowing one or two halves per person.

Remove the rind of the Camembert if it is very hard and cut the cheese into 14 mm (½ in) cubes. Put the cheese in a small saucepan with two tablespoons of the cream and a little lemon juice. Melt the cheese over a very low heat, stirring constantly. When the cheese begins to run, add the remainder of the cream and mix well until the sauce is thick and smooth. Taste and add a little more lemon juice if necessary. Pour the sauce over the pears and sprinkle with a little paprika to decorate. Serve either warm or cold.

VERY GOOD MOIST FRUIT CAKE

Bumble Ogilvy-Wedderburn   *ADC ACCUTRAC*

Bumble says that if you wrap this cake in aluminium foil and hide it at the bottom of a really inaccessible locker, it will keep. However, because it is so good, it tends to get eaten extremely quickly!

MAKES 1 LARGE CAKE

900 g (2 lb) mixed dried fruit

225 g (8 oz) butter or margarine, diced

450 g (1 lb) dark brown sugar

½–1 teaspoon ground mixed spice

500 ml (18 fl oz) cold water

3 large eggs

340 g (12 oz) self-raising flour

2 tablespoons whisky

Put the fruit, butter, sugar, spice and water into a large saucepan, bring to the boil and simmer for about 10–15 minutes. Remove from the heat and allow to cool. When cool, add the eggs, beating well. Fold in the flour and add a little more water, if necessary, to make a consistency that will drop from the spoon. Lastly, stir in the whisky.

Turn the mixture into a buttered and lined 20-cm (8-in) in diameter round cake tin. Bake in a preheated moderate oven (160°C/325°F, gas mark 3) for about 1–1½ hours. The cake is cooked when a knife plunged into the centre comes out clean. Leave the cake to cool in its tin for 10 minutes before turning it out onto a wire rack.

GOLLYWOBBLERS' SPICED FRUIT CAKE

Anne Frazer   *GOLLYWOBBLER*

A gollywobbler is a huge, lightweight sail which is usually set between the fore and main mast of a schooner-rigged yacht. It is not the sort of sail the average cruising yachtsman would set as he sails gently towards his next port of call as this sail requires a team of gorillas with long arms to rig it. This cake is their staple diet and it may be all they are allowed during the race.

MAKES 1 LARGE CAKE

450 g (1 lb) plain flour
225 g (8 oz) mixed dried fruit
  (e.g. sultanas, seedless raisins,
  currants, chopped candied
  peel)
55 g (2 oz) crystallized ginger,
  chopped
110 g (4 oz) walnuts, chopped
110 g (4 oz) dates, chopped

225 g (8 oz) caster sugar
2 teaspoons ground ginger
2 teaspoons ground mixed spice
225 g (8 oz) butter or margarine
4 tablespoons golden syrup
2 eggs, beaten
150 ml (¼ pint) milk
1 teaspoon bicarbonate of soda
a pinch of salt

Mix together all the dry ingredients, apart from the bicarbonate, in a large bowl. In a small saucepan melt together the butter and syrup on a low heat. Pour this mixture gradually into the dry ingredients, stirring constantly. Add the eggs and the bicarbonate of soda dissolved in the milk. Stir well to make a consistency that will drop from the spoon. Turn the mixture into a greased and lined 23-cm (9-in) in diameter round cake tin. Place in the centre of a preheated moderate oven (160°C/325°F, gas mark 3) and bake for about 1½–2 hours. The cake is cooked when a sharp pointed knife plunged into the centre of the cake comes out clean. Leave the cake to cook in its tin for a few minutes before turning it out on to a wire rack. Store in an airtight container.

PARKIN

This should be made at least two days in advance. It is delicious eaten with a slice of full-flavoured cheese and keeps very well if it is put on a thick slice of bread and wrapped in aluminium foil.

MAKES 20 SQUARES APPROX.

170 g (6 oz) self-raising flour	110 g (4 oz) butter or margarine
1 tablespoon soft brown sugar	450 g (1 lb) black treacle
1 teaspoon ground ginger	2 tablespoons milk
1 teaspoon ground mixed spice	55 g (2 oz) slivered almonds
pinch of salt	1 piece of stem ginger, drained of
340 g (12 oz) medium oatmeal	syrup and thinly sliced

Sift the flour, sugar, ginger, spice and salt into a large bowl and mix in the oatmeal. Cut the butter into small dice, put in a small pan with the treacle and milk and melt the ingredients over a low heat. Pour this mixture gradually into the dry ingredients, stirring constantly, to make a soft consistency.

Grease and flour the bottom of a 23 × 30 cm (9 × 12 in) baking dish and line it with buttered greaseproof paper. Bake in a preheated moderate oven (180°C/350°F, gas mark 4) for 15 minutes, then sprinkle the top with the almonds and sliced ginger. Return to the oven for a further 25–30 minutes, or until the top is firm to the touch. Allow the cake to cool in its tin. Cut into about 20 squares and store in an airtight container.

FUDGE BROWNIES

Anne Hammick *WRESTLER OF LEIGH*

These are very popular and leftovers also make a perfect base for trifle.

MAKES 20 SQUARES APPROX.

110 g (4 oz) butter or margarine	55 g (2 oz) plain flour
225 g (8 oz) soft brown sugar	½ teaspoon baking powder
2 eggs	30 g (1 oz) cocoa
1 teaspoon vanilla essence	1 tablespoon milk

Cream together the butter and sugar until the mixture is light and fluffy. Add the eggs and vanilla essence, a little at a time, beating well between each addition. Sift together the flour, baking powder and cocoa and fold them into the creamed mixture together with the milk.

Line a buttered 23 × 30 cm (9 × 12 in) baking tray with well-buttered aluminium foil and bake in a preheated moderate oven (160°C/325°F, gas mark 3) for about 30–35 minutes, or until golden brown on top.

BLACKJACKS

Pat Pocock   *BLACKJACK*

Extra special flapjacks!

MAKES 42

450 g (1 lb) margarine
340 g (12 oz) granulated sugar
3 tablespoons cocoa

3 tablespoons golden syrup
450 g (1 lb) porridge oats

Melt the margarine in a large saucepan and mix in the sugar, cocoa and golden syrup. Remove from the heat and stir in the oats. Mix well. Spread the mixture in a well-buttered shallow 20 × 30 cm (8 × 12 in) tin and bake in a preheated moderate oven (160°C/325°F, gas mark 3) for about 20 minutes or until the biscuits are golden brown. Remove from the oven and allow the biscuits to cool in their tins for a few minutes before turning them out onto a wire rack. Cut into 21 pieces in each tin. Stored in an airtight container, they will keep well.

SCONES

Naomi James   *EXPRESS CRUSADER*

Naomi says that she eats to satisfy her hunger pangs rather than because of any great love of good food. During her epic single-handed Round the World voyage in 1977 she did experiment with a scone mixture to which she added garlic and jam. However, she says the result was pretty disgusting!

This recipe for old-fashioned scones is very suitable for making on board as they can be cooked either in the oven or on top of the stove in a heavy frying pan which has been lightly greased with oil.

MAKES ABOUT 20

450 g (1 lb) plain flour
2½ teaspoons baking powder
55 g (2 oz) butter or margarine
30 g (1 oz) sugar

55 g (2 oz) mixed dried fruit
   (optional)
300 ml (½ pint) milk,
   approximately

Sift the flour and baking powder into a large bowl. Cut the butter or margarine into small dice and rub it into the flour mixture, using your fingertips, until the mixture resembles fine breadcrumbs. Add the sugar and, if you are using it, dried fruit, and mix lightly with a spoon. Gradually add the milk and blend to a soft, moist dough.

Turn the dough onto a lightly-floured surface and knead it for a few minutes until the dough is soft and pliable. Roll out to a thickness of no less than 2 cm (¾ in) and cut into triangles or circles with a floured sharp knife. You should get about 18–20 depending on the thickness – use up all the cuttings.

Either bake the scones on a floured baking tray in a preheated hot oven (220°C/425°F, gas mark 7) for 10 minutes, or on top of the stove in a lightly greased, heavy frying pan for about 7–10 minutes, turning once. The scones should be well risen and brown.

FRYING PAN BREAD

Libby Purves   *BARNACLE GOOSE*

SERVES 4 (or 3 GANNETS)

225 g (8 oz) wholemeal flour	**30 g (1 oz) butter**
225 g (8 oz) plain flour	**a little milk**
2 teaspoons sugar	
1 teaspoon salt	**oil for frying**
pinch of bicarbonate of soda (not essential)	

Mix together the flour, sugar, salt and bicarbonate of soda in a large bowl. Lightly rub in the butter, using your fingertips, until the mixture resembles fine breadcrumbs. Add the milk and mix to a soft dough.

Turn the dough onto a lightly-floured surface and roll into a circle about 2.5 cm (1 in) in thickness. Place a frying pan over a moderate heat and brush lightly with a little oil. When the pan is really hot, put the dough into the pan and cook for about 10 minutes on each side rather like a very fat pancake.

BEAUFORT WIND SCALE 7-12

Moderate Gales to Hurricanes

BOILED EGGS AND PORRIDGE

Des Sleightholme   *GLAD RETURN*

Des is the editor of *Yaching Monthly*, and creator of that irresistible character 'Old Harry'. When I asked him if he would like to contribute to this book, I received the following succinct reply. Whether or not Old Harry had a hand in the matter, I would not like to say!

I go into ecstasies over corned dog hash and swoon
outright over boiled jam duff
I've never been
one for *haute cuisine*
my recipes merit no trumpet
Gale force forage is boiled eggs and porridge
Eat it, like it or lump it

SQUASHED EGG

Clare Francis   *NIGHT SKY*

Clare insists that she is no cook and says this is one of her regular dishes when sailing for breakfast, lunch, tea or supper whether flat calm or a howling gale. It takes little time to prepare, uses minimal equipment (thus saving on the washing up), and is a perfect hot dish to eat single-handed.

SERVES 1

25 g (1 oz) butter	**1 egg**
1 slice of bread	**salt and pepper**

Melt the butter in a frying pan until it foams. Punch a large hole in the middle of the bread and add both to the pan. Fry for a few moments, break the egg into the hole and season well with salt and pepper. Place the cut-out circle on top and press down firmly. Fry gently for 1 minute, turn over and fry for a further minute. Serve immediately.

POPEYE SOUP

The ready-made croûtons now available in most supermarkets go particularly well with this easy and delicious soup.

SERVES 4

300 ml (½ pint) milk	**salt and pepper**
300 ml (½ pint) chicken stock	**pinch of nutmeg**
400 g (14 oz) tin of spinach purée	
a little lemon juice	**croûtons**

Put the milk and stock into a saucepan and add the spinach. Bring to the boil, stirring constantly, reduce the heat and simmer gently for about 5 minutes. Check the seasoning (it may need a little more salt), stir in the lemon juice and sprinkle with the nutmeg and croûtons.

FISH FILLING

John Martin   *MAINSTAY VOORTREKKA*

SERVES 1

1 medium tin of fish (sardines, tuna or mackerel)	**1 small onion, chopped**
	tomato ketchup
1–2 tomatoes, chopped *or* 1 small tin of tomatoes, drained	**Worcestershire sauce**
	mayonnaise

Mash together the fish, tomatoes and onion in a bowl. Add a dash of tomato ketchup, Worcestershire sauce and mayonnaise. Serve either on biscuits or use as a sandwich filling.

TOASTED CHEESE SARNIES

Anne Frazer   *GOLLYWOBBLER*

Toasted 'sarnies' must be one of the most popular and versatile of yachtsmen's fare. They can be made with an assortment of fillings and served as a meal in themselves or as a snack for the dogwatch as well as being the eternal stand-by for voracious crews! If you don't have a grill on board, the sandwiches can be fried on top of the stove without the addition of any fat.

SERVES 1

2 slices of bread *or* 1 whole pitta
   bread
a little butter
1–2 teaspoons French mustard

mango chutney *or* lime pickle
1 large tomato, sliced
30–55 g (1–2 oz) cheese, sliced

If using bread, toast the bread lightly on one side only. Butter the toasted side and spread with mustard, chutney or pickle, cover with the tomato and then top with the cheese. Sandwich the two halves together and toast uncooked sides until each side is golden brown and the cheese is melted.

    If using pitta bread, slit open down one side with a knife and butter inside. Spread with mustard, chutney or pickle and fill with tomato and cheese slices. Press together and place under a preheated hot grill. Toast until each side is golden brown and the cheese is melted.

TIDDY OGGIE

Bumble Ogilvy-Wedderburn   *ADC ACCUTRAC*

Bumble was the cook aboard *ADC Accutrac*, skippered by Clare Francis, in the 1977–78 Round the World Race. She was cooking for a crew of 12 who were unanimous in their praise of her cooking.

SERVES 4–6

450 g (1 lb) shortcrust pastry
   (see page 39)
For the filling:
450 g (1 lb) tinned meat (minced
   beef or stew)

340 g (12 oz) tin of sweetcorn,
   drained
425 g (15 oz) tin of tomatoes
2 onions, finely chopped
salt and pepper

Divide the pastry in two and roll out one piece slightly larger than a buttered square 20 cm (8 in) tin. Line the tin with the pastry. Mix together the meat, sweetcorn, tomatoes and their juice and onions and season well. You can use any leftovers from the galley for this. Spoon the filling into the pastry case. Roll out the remaining pastry large enough to cover the pie. Dampen the pastry rim and cover the pie with the pastry top. Press round the edges to seal.

Bake in a preheated moderately hot oven (200°C/400°F, gas mark 6), then reduce the temperature to cool (150°C/300°F, gas mark 2) and bake for a further 20 minutes.

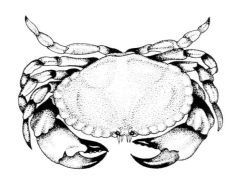

VEGETARIAN SCONE PIE

Maralyn Bailey   *AURALYN II*

Maurice and Maralyn Bailey spent four months adrift in the Pacific Ocean in a life raft after their boat was sunk. Apart from designing their next boat, it is hardly surprising that food was one of their main topics of conversation. Maralyn has also written a cookery book called *The Galley Handbook*.

SERVES 4

450 g (1 lb) tin of mixed vegetables
   or cooked leftover vegetables
425 g (15 oz) tin of vegetable soup
140 g (5 oz) self-raising flour *or*
   plain flour and ½ teaspoon
   baking powder

30 g (1 oz) butter or margarine
2 tablespoons milk

If you are using cooked, leftover vegetables, chop them finely. If using a tin of mixed vegetables, drain them carefully. Put the vegetables into a buttered pie dish. Stir in the tin of vegetable soup.

Sift the flour and baking powder, if you are using it, into a bowl. Cut the fat into small dice and rub it into the flour mixture, using your fingertips, until the mixture resembles fine breadcrumbs. Mix in enough of the milk to blend to a firm dough.

Turn the dough onto a lightly-floured surface and roll out a circle for the lid slightly larger than the pie dish and about 14 mm (½ in) in thickness. Dampen the pie dish rim and cover the pie with the pastry top. Press round the edges to seal. Cook in a preheated moderately hot oven (200°C/400°F, gas mark 6) for 20 minutes or until the pastry is golden brown.

SALMON KEDGEREE

Bumble Ogilvy-Wedderburn   *ADC ACCUTRAC*

Kedgeree was introduced into this country from India during the days of the Empire and was originally served as a breakfast dish but it has since become so popular that it can be served at almost any meal. Although the most familiar version is made with smoked haddock, it is very good made with fresh or tinned salmon, white fish or tuna. Kedgeree freezes extremely well but if you do freeze it, don't add the hard-boiled eggs until later.

SERVES 4

2 200 g (7 oz) tins of salmon *or* tuna   30 g (1 oz) butter or margarine
225 g (8 oz) long grain rice   salt and pepper
3 medium hard-boiled eggs,
   chopped

Cook the rice in plenty of boiling water for about 10–12 minutes and drain carefully through a sieve as soon as it is tender. (If you have room in the saucepan hard-boil the eggs with the rice, otherwise hard-boil them in another pan.)

Melt the butter or margarine in the pan, add the salmon and its juice and cook gently for 3–4 minutes. Add the drained rice to the pan and mix well. Cook over a low heat until the kedgeree is heated through. Just before serving stir in the chopped hard-boiled eggs. Check the seasoning and serve immediately.

TUNA RISOTTO

Rachael Hayward *LOIWING*

This dish is a great stand-by and is just as tasty cold as it is hot. Stirred into scrambled eggs or folded into an omelette it uses up all the leftovers and can be made in a hurry.

SERVES 2–4

200 g (7 oz) tin of tuna in oil *or*
    salmon, flaked
4 medium onions, chopped
1–2 cloves garlic, chopped
110 g (4 oz) long grain rice

pinch of mixed dried herbs
300 ml (½ pint) cold water
vermouth *or* **white wine**
salt and pepper

Drain the oil from the tuna or salmon into a saucepan and add the onions and garlic. Cook gently over a low heat until the onions are soft. Add the rice, increase the heat and fry for a few minutes, stirring constantly, until the rice is transparent. Add the herbs, water and a dash of vermouth or white wine, bring the rice to the boil, reduce the heat to low and cover the pan.

Simmer for about 15–20 minutes or until all the water is absorbed and the rice quite tender. Check from time to time that the rice is not sticking to the pan and add a little more water if necessary. Just before serving, check the seasoning and stir in the flaked tuna. Mix well.

TUNA FISH CRUMBLE

Ann Frazer *GOLLYWOBBLER*

This makes a delicious dish at any time and is simple enough and quick to make in rough weather. Tuna in either oil or brine can be used although Ann says that tuna in brine makes less of a mess on the cabin sole and doesn't turn it into quite the skating rink that tuna in oil does.

SERVES 2

200 g (7 oz) tin of tuna fish *or*
    salmon, drained
285 g (10 oz) tin of condensed
    mushroom soup thinned with
    about 100 ml (4 fl oz) milk
1 medium-sized packet of plain
    crisps

200 g (7 oz) tin of mushrooms, drained
4 tablespoons instant potato
    made up with 275 ml (9 fl oz) boiling
    water
Parmesan cheese
a little butter

Mix together in a bowl the tuna fish and condensed soup which has been thinned with the milk. Crush the crisps and stir with the mushrooms into the fish mixture. Pour the fish mixture into a buttered ovenproof dish, make up the instant potato and spoon the topping over the fish mixture.

Bake in a preheated moderate oven (180°C/350°F, gas mark 4) for about 20 minutes. If you do not have an oven, then pour the fish mixture and topping into the grill pan and cook on top of the stove for a few minutes. Brown the topping by placing it under a preheated hot grill.

HAMBURGERS

Bumble Ogilvy-Wedderburn   *ADC ACCUTRAC*

SERVES 4

450 g (1 lb) fresh minced beef
3 slices of stale bread, crusts
    removed
2 medium onions, finely chopped
1–2 cloves garlic, crushed with a
    little salt
1 teaspoon mixed dried herbs

1 dessertspoon Worcestershire
    sauce
1 egg, lightly beaten
2 tablespoons plain flour *or*
    oatmeal

oil for frying

Put the bread in a bowl and add enough water to cover. Squeeze the bread dry. Mix together the minced beef, onions, garlic, bread, herbs and Worcestershire sauce in a large bowl. Stir in enough of the egg to make a soft but not sticky mixture. Divide the mixture into 4 portions and shape each into a flat round, about 2.5 cm (1 in) thick.

Coat each hamburger in the flour or oatmeal and fry in a little oil for 8–10 minutes, turning once. Serve immediately with sauté potatoes and a salad.

Variation: To turn hamburgers into meatballs with a difference:

4 hamburgers
2 tablespoons oil
1 medium onion, finely chopped
425 g (15 oz) tin of tomato *or*
** mushroom soup**

1 teaspoon mixed dried herbs
grated cheese

Heat 1 tablespoon of the oil in a saucepan, add the onion and cook gently until it is soft, but not browned. Add the soup and herbs. Bring to the boil, reduce the heat and simmer gently.

Shape the hamburgers into meatballs a little bigger than the size of a golf ball. Heat a tablespoon of oil in a frying pan, add the meatballs and brown quickly on all sides. Remove them with a slotted spoon and add to the soup mixture. Simmer very gently (otherwise they will fall apart) for about 20 minutes. Serve with the grated cheese.

POCKET MINCE

Eve Bonham   *HELLO WORLD*

Eve and Diana Thomas-Ellen sailed *Hello World* in the 1982 Twostar, two-handed Transatlantic race.

SERVES 2
425 g (15 oz) tin of minced beef
140 g (5 oz) tin of mushrooms,
** drained**
140 g (5 oz) tin of sweetcorn and
** peppers**

1 teaspoon curry powder
pinch of chilli powder *or* **Tabasco**
** sauce**
2 pitta bread

Empty the tins into a saucepan and add the curry powder, chilli or Tabasco. Mix well. Bring up to boiling point, reduce the heat, cover the pan and simmer for about 15–20 minutes. Stir from time to time to prevent the mixture from sticking or burning.

Warm the pitta bread under the grill or in the oven and slit open down one side. Spoon the mince into the two 'pockets' and serve immediately. There are no plates, no cutlery, only the saucepan to wash up.

FRIGHTFULLY SIMPLE

Robin Knox-Johnston   *SUHAILI*

Robin is extremely modest about his sailing achievements and not least about his epic non-stop Round the World single-handed voyage in *Suhaili*. When I asked him for a recipe or two he replied: 'At last, a subject upon which I consider myself something of an expert! My recipes for very calm, under way, storm force conditions, a weekend and so on are, stew, stew and more stew.'

'It really is most frightfully simple. Open up an interesting selection of tins: bully beef or the like; peas; beans; potatoes; baked beans (the sauce in baked beans helps to give the juice substance); tomatoes; onions; one clove of garlic; stock cubes; salt water and pepper; and then stew well. A good stew gets better the longer it is allowed to exist. I have produced this stew single-handed and when sailing with 16 crew. The best I have ever "created" was in the 1981 Twostar. Billy King Harman and I had been given a lot of fresh steak but the dry ice evaporated within two days. Rather than waste the steak I chopped it all up and made a huge stew with it. It lasted 13 days and could have lasted longer.'

'The main advantages of a stew are that it is easy to make, easy to digest, very sustaining and the flavour can be changed daily.'

Here then is the recipe:

SERVES 1 OR MORE AD INFINITUM

900 g (2 lb) stewing or braising steak
2–3 tablespoons oil
3 large onions, roughly chopped
2 cloves garlic, chopped
2 large carrots, diced
450 g (1 lb) tin of tomatoes
600 ml (1 pint) beef stock

450 g (1 lb) tin of baked beans
450 g (1 lb) tin of peas, drained
200 g (7 oz) tin of mushrooms, drained
450 g (1 lb) tin of potatoes, drained
black pepper
a little red wine (optional)

Cut the steak into large cubes. Heat the oil in a pressure cooker, add the meat, onions and garlic and cook over a moderate heat until the meat begins to brown. Add the carrots, tomatoes and their juice and pour over enough stock to cover the meat. Clamp on the lid and cook according to the manufacturer's instructions on high pressure for about 20 minutes. Release the pressure quickly by either plunging it into a bucket of cold sea water or with the automatic release if you have one. It is important to remember to turn off the flame when the timer rings.

Add the contents of the remaining tins to the pan and mix well. Check the seasoning and add a little red wine if you are using it. Either reheat gently and serve immediately or clamp on the lid and let the stew 'rest' until needed.

The next day add curry powder and a tin of chicken curry or perhaps meat balls and kidney beans – the possibilities are endless!

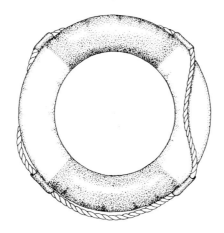

FORCE SEVEN ONE-POT WONDER

Liz Hammick   *WRESTLER OF LEIGH*

SERVES 4

225 g (8 oz) fresh minced beef *or*
   225 g (8 oz) tin of minced beef
oil
1 large onion, chopped
2 large carrots, chopped
2 large potatoes, diced

200 g (7 oz) tin of tomatoes
1 teaspoon tomato purée
150 ml (¼ pint) beef stock
pinch of mixed dried herbs
salt and pepper

Clamp the pressure cooker to the stove. Heat a little oil in the pan, add the onion and fry until it is soft, but not browned. If using fresh mince, add to the pan and fry a little more quickly to brown the meat. If using tinned meat, stir in the contents and fry for a few minutes only. Add the carrots, potatoes, tin of tomatoes, purée, beef stock and sprinkle over the herbs and seasonings.

Clamp on the lid, and cook on high pressure for about 5 minutes. Release the pressure slowly. Serve to crew in bowls sitting on the cabin sole! If there are any leftovers the night watch can add a little more water and reboil and the result is a very tasty soup.

BALLAST

Andrew Bray   *FOOTLOOSE*

Andrew is the deputy editor of *Yachting Monthly* but he also finds time to compete in a number of single- and two-handed races. When I asked him for a suggestion for the rough weather section of recipes he told me that he relies on a particular brand of dehydrated food which he prefers to other types. If it is too rough to even fry an onion, he uses dehydrated onion flakes instead. He recommends that you add your own favourite spices and flavourings to the 'goo' below, such as chilli, turmeric, garlic, curry powder or whatever.

The goo should be cooked until it is a good sticky consistency, sticky enough to stick to your fork and your plate. Andrew advises that in really nasty weather you should leave some goo in the bottom of your pressure cooker as firstly it will provide ballast to stop the pan (and probably your boat) from capsizing and secondly it will form the basis of the next day's stew. After eating the goo, pudding should comprise dried apricots, followed by a good dose of Milk of Magnesia!

SERVES 1

30 g (1 oz) butter	30 g (1 oz) rice *or* pasta shells
1 medium onion, chopped	120 ml (4 fl oz) cold water
1 packet of dehydrated food with enough water to rehydrate – follow instructions on the packet	

Melt the butter in a pressure cooker or heavy saucepan, add the onion and fry until soft. Add the dehydrated food and enough water to rehydrate it. Bring to the boil, reduce the heat and simmer for about 20 minutes. Add whatever flavourings or spices catch your imagination, stir in the rice or pasta and the remainder of the water. Cook for a further 15–20 minutes, or until sufficiently solid. Serve in a high-sided or deep bowl and eat before it sets!

QUICK BEAN STEW

Mike Scneideman   *DIVIRTIMENTI*

This is a quick version of the bean stews and cassoulets of France. Mike assures me that he once cooked this in the Australian outback in his billycan. However, it is extremely good on a cold night in the English Channel!

SERVES 1–2

15 g (½ oz) dehydrated mushrooms	200 g (7 oz) tin of tomatoes
85 g (3 oz) smoked streaky bacon, thick cut	120 ml (4 fl oz) red wine
1 medium onion, sliced	450 g (1 lb) tin of red kidney beans, drained
2 cloves garlic, chopped	

Put the mushrooms in a cup and pour over enough boiling water to cover and leave it to soak. Cut the bacon into narrow strips about 14 mm (½ in) thick and put them, without additional fat, into a pan. Cook on a low to moderate heat until the fat begins to run. Add the onion and garlic and cook until the bacon is crisp and the onion soft and just beginning to brown.

Stir in the tin of tomatoes and their juice, wine, and the strained juice from the mushrooms. Increase the heat and boil quickly until the liquid has reduced by about two-thirds. Add the kidney beans and mushrooms and cook for a few minutes longer until the beans are heated through.

BOILED RICE

John Ridgeway and Andy Briggs   *ENGLISH ROSE VI*

John Ridgeway and Andy Briggs set off from Ardmore – where John has run his well-known and successful School of Adventure for a number of years – on a non-stop round the world voyage via the five great Capes. Their target was to accomplish it in less than 208 days as they both had to be back at Ardmore to start the 1984 instructors' course. They completed the voyage in 205 days which is what you might call timing.

SERVES 2–4

225 g (8 oz) long grain rice   **1 teaspoon salt**
30 g (1 oz) butter or margarine   **1 bay leaf**
750 ml (1¼ pints) cold water

Melt the butter or margarine in a saucepan which has a well-fitting lid and add the rice. Stir the rice in the fat until it is well coated and fry gently until the rice is transparent. Add the cold water, salt and bay leaf. Bring the rice to the boil, reduce the heat to low and cover the pan. Simmer for about 15 minutes or until all the water is absorbed. It is important not to remove the lid during the cooking. Fish out the bay leaf and serve.

Variation: This makes a good alternative to plain boiled rice, is delicious used as a stuffing for green peppers and also makes a very good vegetarian meal.
    Prepare the rice exactly as above but about halfway through the cooking time add:

1 red or green pepper, deseeded   **30 g (1 oz) raisins**
** and chopped**   **30 g (1 oz) salted peanuts or**
110 g (4 oz) mushrooms, sliced   ** almonds**

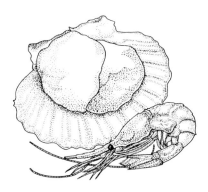

SAVOURY MASH

Chris Butler *ACHILLEA*

Chris designs and builds production yachts which he tests himself by taking part in long-distance, single-handed races. Despite being seven hours late over the starting line in the 1984 OSTAR, he still managed to win Class V, a highly creditable performance. This recipe is his way of 'cheering up' dehydrated potato as an accompaniment to any meat dish or even to eat on its own.

SERVES 1–2

30 g (1 oz) butter or margarine	**150 ml (¼ pint) milk**
1 large onion, chopped	**1 measure potato powder**
400 g (14 oz) tin of green beans,	**1 egg**
drained	**salt and pepper**

Melt the butter or margarine in a saucepan, add the onion and fry gently until it is browned, but without allowing it to burn. Add the beans and the milk and bring up to the boil. Sprinkle with the potato powder and mix well. Remove from the heat. Crack the egg into the mixture, beat well and add a little more butter. Season well and serve immediately.

SELF-RAISING FLOUR BREAD

Richard Clifford *WARRIOR SHAMAAL*

This really is a type of pitta bread. Quick and easy to make even in the worst kind of weather, split it open while still warm and stuff with cheese, cold fish or meat or any other mixture. It makes a very sustaining meal.

SERVES 1

225 g (8 oz) self-raising flour	**3–4 tablespoons sea water**

Put the flour into a large bowl and add enough water to make a fairly stiff dough. Knead with your hands until the dough leaves the sides of the bowl clean. Knead well on a lightly-floured surface until soft and pliable. Flatten the dough and place under a preheated hot grill. Cook for 7–8 minutes turning once.

BREAD BAKED IN A SAUCEPAN

Richard Clifford   *WARRIOR SHAMAAL*

175 ml (6 fl oz) sea water	**450 g (1 lb) plain flour**
2 tablespoons dried yeast	**a little oil**
1 teaspoon sugar	**asbestos mat**

Heat the water to about blood temperature (37°C/98°F). If you cannot measure the temperature accurately it is better to err on the cool side. Mix the yeast and sugar in a jug or small bowl with half of the warm water. Leave the mixture to stand in a warm place for about 30 minutes until the yeast dissolves and the liquid becomes frothy.

Put the flour into a large bowl and gradually add the yeast liquid, stirring constantly. Slowly add the remaining warm water and mix to a fairly stiff dough.

Turn the dough onto a lightly-floured surface and knead it for about 15 minutes, or until the dough is soft and pliable. Form it into a ball. Lightly brush the dough with oil and put it inside a large plastic bag and leave it to double in size in a warm place. This can take from 2–6 hours depending on the temperature.

When the dough is well risen, punch it down and knead it again lightly. Thoroughly oil the inside of a heavy saucepan and place it on the asbestos mat over a very low heat. Cook for 30–40 minutes, then turn once and cook for a further 30–40 minutes. (It may not be necessary to use the asbestos mat until about halfway through the cooking time, but take care not to allow the bottom of the saucepan or the bread to burn.)

THE INFAMOUS HOT TODDY

Geoff Hales   *QUEST FOR CHARITY*

One measure should be taken at 05.00 hours when the skipper is showing signs of suffering from the cold and wet and the wind-speed indicator is registering 40 knots or more. If one dose is insufficient to reduce the wind speed, then a second may be taken at approximately 05.30 hours and a speedy recovery is guaranteed – well almost.

FOR EACH SERVING

⅓ glass dark naval rum   ⅓ glass grapefruit *or* lemon
⅓ glass boiling water   squash, undiluted

Put the rum and squash into a tumbler and top up with the boiling water. Stir and serve.

EGG NOG

Laurel Holland

This is a very nourishing drink and very useful for children and adults who are slightly off-colour and don't feel like eating a meal. It is good hot or cold.

FOR EACH SERVING

1 egg   a little vanilla essence
150 ml (¼ pint) milk   grated nutmeg (optional)
1 tablespoon sugar

Put all the ingredients in a bowl and whisk with a fork or rotary whisk.

SEA FALCON SPECIAL

Geoff Hales   *QUEST FOR CHARITY*

Geoff dreamed up this interesting little number while making a cold autumn passage with Robin Knox-Johnston in his catamaran *Sea Falcon*. In that boat beef extract was the standard night-watch's drink. One night, while making this for his middle watch partner, he spied the pickled onion jar and wondered if the addition of an onion or two might add a certain something, particularly if it was not discovered until taking the final swig with the mug well upraised. The initial comment was that the drink tasted much nicer than usual and at the last gulp he got the solid mouthful. When Robin recovered from the shock he said he actually enjoyed it.

   If offering this drink as a surprise, choose large onions which cannot be swallowed whole.

FOR EACH SERVING

1 teaspoon beef extract   **boiling water**
1 pickled onion, or more, to taste

Put the beef extract and onion into a mug and top up with boiling water. Stir until the extract has dissolved and serve.

HELMSMAN'S BREW

Robin Gamble   *ASTERISK*

Robin tells me that he concocted this brew during the delivery trip in his newly-acquired yacht. It was a cold night in early March and a fresh wind was blowing snow showers across the deck as they made their way towards the North Hinder Light. Freezing spray added to the discomfort of the night-watch on deck while, down below, torchlight was all the skipper/navigator/cook had to see with as he crouched over the stove trying to warm himself up.

SERVES 4

1 mug of water per person, mostly   **2 tablespoons syrup**
   fresh   **1 tablespoon sugar**
400 g (14 oz) tin of condensed   **whisky to taste**
   milk
110 g (4 oz) chocolate, broken into
   squares

Put the water, milk, chocolate, syrup and sugar into a pan. Slowly bring to the boil, stirring constantly, reduce the heat and simmer gently until the chocolate has melted. Ladle the liquid into mugs and as you hand them up on deck, add a splash of whisky to each.

FASTNET FORTIFIER

David Gay   *SARIE MARAIS*

During the 1977 Fastnet Race David and his crew were totally becalmed for long periods of time. On about the third day out a near disaster struck – they ran out of gas and David discovered that the spare cannister was empty. However, being extremely resourceful, David proceeded to convert his stove to 'candle power' with some candles he had on board.

Should you find yourself in the same position, this is how you do it: Cut the cardboard core of a kitchen roll into sections. Melt down some candles and remove the wick. Cut the wick in half and tie onto pencils, then pour the liquid wax into the cardboard rolls. Balance the pencils across the top, making sure that the wick is touching the bottom so that they are similar to old-fashioned night-lights. Place these night-lights under each burner and the stove can then be used as normal except for the grill and oven. Of course, it will take longer and the galley will be covered in thick black soot but that is much better than living on cold food as David's crew will testify!

SERVES 6

1.75 litres (3 pints) fresh water	**1 dash of sherry per mug**
3 beef stock cubes	**1 dry biscuit per person**

Bring the water and stock cubes to the boil in a large saucepan, stirring constantly to dissolve the cubes. Ladle into mugs, and add a slug of sherry just before serving.

HANDY MEASURES

Although grams and ounces have been specified in the recipes, few of you will keep kitchen scales on board so here are some handy measures which, with your own experienced judgement, will help you guess the weights more accurately.

3 teaspoons = 1 tablespoon
16 tablespoons = 1 cup
1 cup = ½ pint

breadcrumbs, fresh	30 g (1 oz)	= approximately	7 level tablespoons
butter	15 g (½ oz)	= ,,	1 tablespoon
cheese, Cheddar, grated	30 g (1 oz)	= ,,	3 level tablespoons
cocoa	30 g (1 oz)	= ,,	3 ,, ,,
cornflour	30 g (1 oz)	= ,,	3 ,, ,,
dried fruit	30 g (1 oz)	= ,,	2 ,, ,,
flour, unsifted	30 g (1 oz)	= ,,	3 ,, ,,
rice, uncooked	30 g (1 oz)	= ,,	2 ,, ,,
rolled oats	30 g (1 oz)	= ,,	4 ,, ,,
sugar, caster, granulated, Demerara	30 g (1 oz)	= ,,	2 ,, ,,
syrup, honey, treacle	30 g (1 oz)	= ,,	1 ,, ,,
liquids	15 ml (½ fl oz) = ,,		1 tablespoon
	60 ml (2 fl oz) = ,,		3 tablespoons
	150 ml (¼ pint) = ,,		8 tablespoons

yeast   1 sachet usually contains 15 g (½ oz) which is sufficient for a 1.5 kg (3.3 lb) loaf
juice of 1 lemon = 2–3 tablespoons
juice of 1 lime = 1–2 tablespoons
unless specified, all eggs are medium or size 3

WEIGHTS AND MEASURES

For all recipes, quantities are given in both metric and Imperial measures. Exact conversion from Imperial to metric measures does not usually give very convenient working quantities and so the metric measures have been rounded off into units of 30 grams. The table below shows the recommended equivalents.

Weights

15 g = ½ oz	170 g = 6 oz	400 g = 14 oz	1.35 kg = 3 lb
20 g = ¾ oz	200 g = 7 oz	425 g = 15 oz	1.8 kg = 4 lb
30 g = 1 oz	225 g = 8 oz	450 g = 1 lb	2.3 kg = 5 lb
55 g = 2 oz	255 g = 9 oz	500 g = 1 lb 2 oz	2.7 kg = 6 lb
85 g = 3 oz	285 g = 10 oz	570 g = 1¼ lb	3.2 kg = 7 lb
100 g = 3½ oz	310 g = 11 oz	680 g = 1½ lb	3.4 kg = 8 lb
110 g = 4 oz	340 g = 12 oz	900 g = 2 lb	4 kg = 9 lb
140 g = 5 oz	370 g = 13 oz	1 kg = 2 lb 3 oz	4.5 kg = 10 lb

Liquid Measures

1 teaspoon (5 ml) = 1 teaspoon	750 ml = 1¼ pints
1 tablespoon (15 ml) = 1 tablespoon	900 ml = 1½ pints
120 ml = 4 fl oz	1 litre = 1¾ pints
150 ml = ¼ pint	1.2 litres = 2 pints
175 ml = 6 fl oz	1.25 litres = 2¼ pints
200 ml = ⅓ pint	1.5 litres = 2½ pints
250 ml = 8 fl oz	1.6 litres = 2¾ pints
300 ml = ½ pint	1.75 litres = 3 pints
350 ml = 12 fl oz	2 litres = 3½ pints
400 ml = 14 fl oz	2.25 litres = 4 pints
450 ml = ¾ pint	2.5 litres = 4½ pints
500 ml = 18 fl oz	2.75 litres = 5 pints
600 ml = 1 pint	

Oven Temperatures

very cool	(110°C/225°F, gas mark ¼)	moderately hot	(190°C/375F, gas mark 5)
	(120°C/250°F, gas mark ½)		(200°C/400°F, gas mark 6)
cool	(140°C/275°F, gas mark 1)	hot	(220°C/425°F, gas mark 7)
	(150°C/300°F, gas mark 2)		(230°C/450°F, gas mark 8)
moderate	(160°C/325°F, gas mark 3)	very hot	(240°C/475°F, gas mark 9)
	(180°C/350°F, gas mark 4)		(250°C/500°F, gas mark 9)

INDEX